Comfort
in the Darkness

The Bible Reading Fellowship
15 The Chambers, Vineyard
Abingdon OX14 3FE
brf.org.uk

BRF is a Registered Charity (233280)

ISBN 978 0 85746 423 1
First published 2016
10 9 8 7 6 5 4 3 2 1 0

Text © Rachel Turner 2016
The author asserts the moral right to be identified as the author of this work

Cover image by Rebecca J Hall

Acknowledgements
Unless otherwise stated, scripture quotations are taken from The Holy Bible, New International
Version (Anglicised edition) copyright © 1979, 1984, 2011 by Biblica. Used by permission of
Hodder & Stoughton Publishers, a Hachette UK company. All rights reserved. 'NIV' is a registered
trademark of Biblica. UK trademark number 1448790.

Scripture taken from the New Century Version®. Copyright © 2005 by Thomas Nelson. Used by
permission. All rights reserved.

Scripture taken from *The Message*. Copyright © 1993, 1994, 1995, 1996, 2000, 2001, 2002. Used by
permission of NavPress Publishing Group.

Scripture quotations taken from the Holy Bible, New Living Translation, copyright © 1996, 2004,
2007, 2013. Used by permission of Tyndale House Publishers, Inc., Carol Stream, Illinois 60188.
All rights reserved.

Every effort has been made to trace and contact copyright owners for material used in this
resource. We apologise for any inadvertent omissions or errors, and would ask those concerned
to contact us so that full acknowledgement can be made in the future.

A catalogue record for this book is available from the British Library

Printed and bound by CPI Group (UK) Ltd, Croydon CR0 4YY

Comfort
in the Darkness

HELPING CHILDREN DRAW CLOSE TO GOD
THROUGH BIBLICAL STORIES OF NIGHT-TIME AND SLEEP

RACHEL TURNER

For my godchildren—Eli, Zeke, Tabby and Emily.
I pray that each of your nights is filled
with the joy of God.

Acknowledgements

Caleb Turner: every day it is a joy to be your mum. We have walked this journey of night-times together. Thank you for sharing hearts with me, praying for me, and teaching me all you know about Daddy God.

My husband, Mark: thank you for being my partner and for enduring with me through all the stages of writing. From the hours of listening to me talk through ideas, or keeping me going in the midst of deep frustration, to just throwing food at me and keeping out of the way of a 'flow', I am deeply grateful to have you in my life.

My mother, Susan Hart: I can never thank you enough for your support, encouragement and faithfulness in my life. Thank you for constantly teaching me and for your time and sacrifice as you added your wisdom to this book.

My dad, Terry Hart: thank you for always making me feel as if everything is accomplishable if I persevere. You inspire me to be a better leader and deeper disciple of Christ.

My editor, Olivia Warburton: thank you for your effortless grace and continuing partnership.

Thank you to all my friends who encouraged me and supported our family while I wrote: Elaine Webster, Will Leaf, Andrea Johnson, Annie and Pete Willmot, Josh Lees, Rachel Norburn, Elliot and Jo Ireton, James and Susie Yeates, and our endless kind community of friends.

Contents

INTRODUCTION...7

1. THE FIRST NIGHT..11

2. GOD'S NIGHT LIGHT...15

3. NIGHTLY SPECIAL DELIVERY...21

4. A VOICE IN THE NIGHT..29

5. SONGS IN THE NIGHT...37

6. AWAKE ALL NIGHT...43

7. NO ORDINARY NIGHT...51

8. OVERNIGHT CHAT...59

9. RESCUE IN THE DARK...67

10. HIDDEN IN THE NIGHT...75

11. SLEEPING IN THE STORM..83

12. MORE REAL THAN REAL..91

13. GIFTS IN THE NIGHT...97

14. A CLUE TO THE FUTURE...105

15. A CHANGE OF HEART...113

16. A NEW KIND OF CALL...121

FAQ...129

Introduction

Night-time. When you say the word 'night-time' to most of us parents or carers, a flood of clashing thoughts pours over us: the joy of cuddles; the stress of wrangling children through the bath and food routine; the endless requests for 'one more' drink, hug, story and question; and the precious conversations dealing with bad dreams, random fears and interrupted sleep. Parenting children in the night isn't easy.

Night-time is such a vulnerable time for our children. It's a time when the worries of the day, deep fears, thoughtful wonderings, and tomorrow's stresses all bubble to the surface. We long for our children to find the deep peace, safety and rest that come from God in the night. We want our children to experience the night-time as a wonderful place of closeness to and connection with us and with God—a place where our children can process their days and rest in contentment.

So often, though, our children struggle in the night. They can be afraid of the dark, uncomfortable with being alone or terrified by nightmares, or they may find it difficult to settle their minds and hearts. So we give them night lights and read them Bible stories and insist that there are no monsters in the closet or ghosts in the hallway. For a while, our plasters may work, but they don't change our children's fears. The night often remains a source of uncertainty, to be managed some times better than others.

Our children need to learn how to think differently about the night. They need to explore who God is in the night and what he does while they sleep and dream. They need to learn to see the night-time as being filled with the good things of God. This book aims to help you take your children on this journey of exploration.

Night-time can be one of the most frustrating times for us as parents, but it can also be one of the most powerful times of parenting as well. It is a time of intimacy, of reflection, of peace and thought. It can be a time of building connections and spiritual foundations. It can be a joy. It's a time for our children to think about God and become rooted in the truth of him in the night—a truth that goes beyond their immediate need and straight to their hearts.

This isn't a book to tell you how to do your night-time routine better. It's not a book to help you make your children into perfect children who never ask for water and always stay in bed. This is a book to help you shape the time at night with your children in a way that connects you to each other and to God, even in the midst of your family's quirkiness and the way they are. It will help you build for your children a foundational understanding of God, so that when they lie down to sleep, they will know who God is in the dark and quietness, and what he does while they are asleep.

There are 16 stories in this book to read to your children. Each story can stand on its own. If you only want to read the stories to your children, then the book will serve your needs. Each story covers a different aspect of who God is in the night.

If you want to go beyond reading the stories, at the end of each one is a section entitled 'Extras for parents'. This section contains suggestions for how to start a conversation with your children or with your whole family about the key truth presented in the story. It also offers a few suggestions of how to use that key truth to pray and to help your children connect with God in new ways. Lastly, it contains brief 'Parenting for faith' tools to help you feel better equipped to talk about God with your children.

Feel free to use the information in the 'Extras for parents' section as much or as little as you like. The extras are just that—extra. A final additional resource is the FAQ section at the back of the book, which may answer some questions about helping children spiritually at night.

Some parents will find it helpful, as they read through the stories, to create something together as a family to remind them of the foundational truths about God that they are exploring each night. If you feel your family would benefit from this, you will find some craft suggestions in the FAQ section (see page 130).

However you choose to use this book, please remember that God has placed you perfectly in your children's lives to help them grow to live connected to him. No one can be as spiritually effective in their lives as he has made you to be, and he will walk with you every step of the way.

My prayer is that your family will go on a wonderful journey of transforming the night into a God-filled experience of him, and that you as a parent will feel confident to parent your children through the night as you do through the day.

May God give you deep sleep, endurance and nights filled with joy and peace.

1

The first night

Genesis 1

with John 1:1–5; Isaiah 40:22; Psalm 102:25

In the beginning was God. Before there was anything, there was God. And he was the same as he is now: wonderful, kind, perfect, powerful, fair, loving and wise. And he was planning. Oh, the plans he was making! Oh, the wonders he was designing! They were beyond anything we could ever dream or imagine.

He waited until the perfect time. The time that was just right. And then… he spoke.

The word of God can make all things happen, and with a few words he began his great creation. 'Let there be light,' God said. And light shone brightly, clear and vibrant.

But God made a choice. God kept darkness, too. He saved it and protected it. He could have got rid of it altogether, but there was something about darkness that was important and special. So he separated the light from the dark. He called the light 'day', and the dark he called 'night'. He had great plans for both.

God's hands stretched out the universe, and he called the stars into their places by name. He built the sky and created the sun and moon to give light to the earth. And with that gift, he gave us time, in days, months and years. This gift of time would bring a pattern to our lives, with our days different from our nights.

God looked at what he had made: night and day, dark and light, moon and stars and sun. And he saw that it was good.

Good, because part of his plans for the world, part of his purposes for his people, and part of the wonders that he was going to bring, were going to happen in the night. And so for each of us, as the moon rises and darkness falls, we can expect wonderful things, because God is in the night-time too.

Extras for parents

Key truth: God made the night and thinks it is good.

Discussion

If you want to discuss this story with your children, here are some suggestions.

First, help your children recognise the key truth from the story. These questions will help you get started:

- What did God create?
- What did God think about what he had made?

You may want to continue the discussion and broaden your children's understanding of the story's key truth. Choose one or two of these questions to launch a conversation and see where it goes:

- What would life without night-time be like?
- What wonderful things do you think we can expect from God at night?
- What is your idea of a perfect night-time for us as a family?

Pray

If you want to pray with your children, here is a prayer that may serve as a starting point.

Father God, thank you for making the night-time. You said that night-time is good, and we want to learn how to love being with you at night. We look forward to all your wonderful plans in the night. Thank you, God.

If you want to help your children connect with God and continue chatting with him on their own, here are a few suggestions. It works best if you make the suggestion and then they chat with God in their minds or whisper into their hands so that you don't hear. Either way, after you've made the suggestion, pause for at least 30 seconds of quiet time to allow your children to connect with God on their own.

- Why don't you tell God one of your favourite things about night-time?
- Tell him what you don't like about night-time.
- Let's ask him to fill our imaginations with what a perfect night-time might be like.

'Parenting for faith' tool

Create a culture of wondering together instead of a culture of finding the right answers. Affirm your children's ponderings, ask follow-up questions and participate in the discussion by sharing your own honest thoughts. Together you can explore the majesty of God and his life with us.

2

God's night light

Exodus 14

Mahlah's heart thumped wildly in the dark as she lay still in the corner of her family's small tent. This was their home now. Outside, the wind continued to whip the tent's thin walls back and forth with a loud slap-slap-slap. Then, something crashed in the distance.

Mahlah felt her little sister Tirzah scoot close to her. 'What is that sound?' Tirzah asked. Her voice was wobbly. 'I don't like the desert.' She shivered and burrowed her face into Mahlah's arm. 'I want to go back to our other home.'

'Oh, little one, we will never go back there.' Mahlah closed her eyes and thought about their old home. So much had happened since their family was woken up in the middle of the night and sent out of Egypt with so many other families. Mahlah knew that Tirzah was too young to really understand what life had been like back there. Their family had been slaves for as long as anyone could remember. They had been forced to work for Pharaoh, the king of Egypt, and they'd been whipped if they didn't do their work fast enough. Mahlah sighed. It seemed like everyone she knew had been a slave. Every day was hard and sad. She never wanted to go back. But what would happen to them now?

Suddenly, a sharp howl pierced the cold night air, somewhere beyond the tent walls. 'We're going to be eaten by wild animals,' Tirzah moaned. 'I just know it.'

Mahlah pulled her sister even closer and hugged her. Mahlah felt fear squeezing her own heart, too. 'Why would God do this?' she thought. 'Why would he rescue us from being hurt as slaves, only to bring us into a desert to be eaten by animals or insects, or to be blown away by the wind?' It just didn't make sense.

Mahlah listened to the wind for a while. She thought back to how God had used his cloud to lead her people to the Red Sea. God had led them, and they had followed. But what about now? If this strong wind had blown God's cloud away, then he would not be there to lead them any more. They would be completely on their own. Mahlah wondered if God's cloud *was* still there. She decided she had to find out.

Mahlah carefully folded back her blanket and shuffled through the deep darkness toward the flap-door of the tent. She ran her fingers up along the tent flap to find a small, familiar hole, and then she leaned in close for a look through it.

What Mahlah saw amazed her. God's massive pillar of cloud was still standing tall between the sprawling camp of her people and the faraway darkness of the empty desert. The furious wind had not moved it. God's pillar of cloud was not only still there; it was brightly blazing as if it were filled with intense fire. God had led them out of Egypt and now he was standing guard over them at night. He hadn't left them. Peace poured into Mahlah's body. A smile spread across her face.

She adjusted the tent door flap to stand open slightly, so that a single beam of light from God's pillar of cloud could stream into the tent. Mahlah dropped to her knees and crawled back toward Tirzah, who was curled under their blanket. She gently touched Tirzah's shoulder. 'Open your eyes, Tirzah. Look! Can you see?'

Tirzah raised her head and squinted at the light shining through the hole and down on to her blanket.

Mahlah sat down, close to her sister. 'That light is from God's cloud, Tirzah. He is still here with us, even in this scary night. He led us here, and he will continue to lead us to our new home.'

Tirzah ran her fingers gently across the beam of light on her blanket.

Mahlah lay down on their bed. 'Remember, back at our old home, we had a little candle as a night light, just in case we were scared?'

Tirzah nodded.

'Well, now we have something better. God is so close to us— he is our night light now.' Both girls smiled and watched the glow of God as they drifted off to sleep, afraid of nothing.

Extras for parents

Key truth: God is close to us through the night.

Discussion

If you want to discuss this story with your children, here are some suggestions.

First, help your children recognise the key truth from the story. These questions will help you get started:

* What was Mahlah feeling at the beginning of the story?
* How could the Israelites see that God was with them?
* Why did Mahlah stop being afraid when she saw God's light shining from the cloud?

You may want to continue the discussion and broaden your children's understanding of the story's key truth. Choose one or two of these questions to launch a conversation and see where it goes:

* Why do you think God wants to be close to people when they are sleeping?
* As a parent, share a story of a time when you felt that God was close to you at night. What did it feel like and how did you know that God was there? What difference did it make? Invite your children to share their stories.
* We can't see God at night in a pillar of fire, like the Israelites did, but he's still that close. Actually, he is even closer to us. How can we remind ourselves that God is super-close at night?

Pray

If you want to pray with your children, here is a prayer that may serve as a starting point.

Father God, thank you for being so close to us in the night-time. It can feel so lonely at night. Please help our hearts to feel your super-closeness and help our minds to know you are right here as we lie in our beds. Thank you, God.

If you want to help your children connect with God and continue chatting with him on their own, here are a few suggestions. It works best if you make the suggestion and then they chat with God in their minds or whisper into their hands so that you don't hear. Either way, after you've made the suggestion, pause for at least 30 seconds of quiet time to allow your children to connect with God on their own.

- Encourage your children to chat with God through drawing or writing. Suggest that they draw a picture for God, showing him what their nights feel like now between them and him. Then ask them to flip the paper over and draw a picture for God of what they want their nights to feel like, together with him. Tell them that as they draw, they can tell God about what they are drawing, in their heads or whispering it out loud.
- Ask them to lie quietly and ask God to be with them as they fall asleep. Wait in silence for 30 seconds for your child to connect with God.

'Parenting for faith' tool

Your experience of life with God is one of the most powerful tools you have to help your children grow spiritually. They need insights into what a normal, not-perfect-yet relationship with God looks like, so that they can learn that God is real and is working in the everyday routines of life. Throughout this book, you will be invited to share your experiences with God as well as encouraging your children to share their experiences.

Do not feel pressured to make up any stories or to feel that your experience isn't good enough. Even to say, 'You know, I'm still on this journey, and I really want to experience this for the first time too. I'm excited' is a really important and powerful thing. Your testimony will always be powerful to your children, and they will feel heard and validated when you listen to theirs.

3

Nightly special delivery

Exodus 16

Iru stepped out of the tent and squinted at the night sky. He had just checked his family's supplies, and he knew they were out of all the food that they had brought with them, to follow God in the desert. He was nervous. Back in Egypt, he always knew where his next meal would come from. The markets were full, the shops had plenty, and his house always had food. His mouth watered, just remembering. Leeks and vegetables and lamb and lentils and fruit, and his favourite sweet cakes, that his grandmother made. Now he was living in a tent surrounded by sand, and he had no idea what his next meal would be.

'Son,' said his mother, poking her head out of the tent, 'don't worry. Do you remember what Moses said at the big meeting? God told him that he is going to bring us plenty of bread to eat in the morning.'

'Yes, Mum. I remember,' said Iru. He turned and gazed at God's huge fiery pillar of cloud, standing bright against the darkness… and he wondered. 'But, *how* will God bring bread for us to eat, way out here in the desert? And do it overnight?'

His mother smiled and joined him outside in the cool evening breeze. 'I don't know, Iru. But I do know that our God never sleeps. Night or day, he will provide what we need.'

She ruffled his hair and kissed the back of his head. 'I guess we'll just have to wait until morning and see.'

Later that evening, Iru lay in bed and listened to the sound of the thousands of people camping all around, settling in for the night. Babies cried, dads sang songs, and old people whispered around their fires, guessing about the bread that God had promised to deliver.

He slowly drifted off to sleep, his heart troubled, wondering how God would bring bread while he slept.

In the morning, a shout from his brother jolted him from his sleep. More shouts erupted outside his tent.

Iru scrambled to throw on his clothes as he stumbled into the blinding morning light, barefoot. Instantly something felt different—slightly wet. What was he standing on? The ground was covered in thin dew… and something else. His eyes adjusted to the light, and he saw that the ground was blanketed with a thin layer of… something he had never seen before. Something no one had ever seen before. 'What is it?' he asked himself.

Iru carefully reached down and touched it, amazed. Up close he could see lots of individual pieces of something white and small, hard and bobbly, beautiful and different.

His mother was sitting on a rock, rolling a pile of the stuff between her fingers. 'Iru, Moses says this is the bread that the Lord has given us to eat. Look at it!' His mother tossed him a jar. 'Here you go, son! Fill it up with as much as you think you will eat today. Come on!'

Iru dropped to his knees and scooped several piles of precious grain into his jar. 'Fill it up with only enough for today?' he asked. 'Shouldn't we gather as much as we can, so that we can eat tomorrow and the next day? Who knows when we will get this again?' Iru filled his jar, and then used both arms and hands to scoop up a large mound of white pieces into his robes. 'I do not want to be hungry ever again!'

'Iru, stop. Stop. IRU! STOP!'

Iru locked eyes with his mother, and he froze with the large scoop of white stuff still in his arms. He could feel his face getting hot.

His mother hurried over and crouched down next to him. She spoke firmly but gently. 'Iru, during the night God provided this food for us to eat today. God said he would provide in the night for our tomorrows—one tomorrow at a time. I trust that.'

Iru looked at his mum's hopeful face and took a deep breath. He opened his arms and let the large mound of white flakes slowly slip from his arms and off his robes.

Throughout the next hour he watched in wonder as the sun slowly melted the leftover flakes on the ground until they disappeared. He watched as people ground up the hard pieces they'd collected, cooked them in pots and made flat pieces of bread with them. He was amazed at the taste of this new food, thick and satisfying with a flicker of honey and fresh oil.

That night as he stared at the setting sun, Iru realised that they had eaten all their food. There was nothing left for tomorrow. But he wasn't afraid or nervous any more. He smiled at God's cloud, beginning to glow in the darkening sky. As he lay down that night, he placed his empty jar by his bed. He smiled a little and closed his eyes, ready for God's next delivery in the night.

Extras for parents

Key truth: God provides for me in the night.

Discussion

If you want to discuss this story with your children, here are some suggestions.

First, help your children recognise the key truth from the story. These questions will help you get started:

- Why was Iru worried about not having food?
- What did God say he was going to do?
- What did the food look and taste like?

You may want to continue the discussion and broaden your children's understanding of the story's key truth. Choose one or two of these questions to launch a conversation and see where it goes:

- Why do you think God told the people only to take enough for the day, not to try to keep loads for the future?
- Has God ever provided for one of your needs overnight? (As a parent, share a story of God providing for you or a person you know. Invite your children to share a story from their life, or a story they have heard.)
- Iru was very worried. Have you ever been worried at night? What about?

Pray

If you want to pray with your children, here is a prayer that may serve as a starting point.

Father God, thank you that you know all of our needs, even before we ask for them. Thank you that you are so powerful that you can provide anything overnight. There are lots of things we need right now, and we trust you to take care of all of them. Help us to trust in you and wake up excited to see what you will provide. Thank you, God.

If you want to use scripture to help your children connect with God, here is one example for you.

Ask your children if there is anything they are worried about or anything they feel they need from God. If you feel you are getting answers about their wants instead of their needs, feel free to focus just on what they are worried about.

Read to them or tell them about these verses in the Bible: 'Don't worry about anything; instead, pray about everything. Tell God what you need, and thank him for all he has done. Then you will experience God's peace, which exceeds anything we can understand. His peace will guard your hearts and minds as you live in Christ Jesus' (Philippians 4:6–7, NLT).

Suggest that you do just what scripture says. Start off by saying, 'Let's all chat to God quietly in our own heads or into our hands and tell him what we are worried about and why.' Allow at least 30 seconds for you all to do that.

Then say, 'Now let's think of a few things we are really thankful for, that God has already done for us. Can you think of those things? OK, now let's tell him quietly by ourselves.' Allow another 30 seconds.

Remind them of the final part of verse 7, about how God's peace will come. Then say something like, 'Let's just wait and be ready for God's peace to come and guard our hearts and minds. Get your hearts and minds ready! Go!' Sit quietly together, waiting on God, for at least 30 seconds. Then wrap up by asking, 'How do you feel now?'

'Parenting for faith' tool

So often, as parents, we deal with our children's worries at night. Helping our children to deal with what is on their hearts is a wonderful part of evenings, because God can provide for our needs at night. Often, when our children ask for things from God, at the heart of their request is a specific need, particularly if they are anxious or worried. Our role as parents is to find out what the deep need is and help them engage with God about it. When a child asks God, 'Stop Johnny from picking on me,' that desire comes out of a deep need to feel safe and be safe at school. Help your child to move beyond the request to really connecting with God about that need: wanting to feel safe, wanting a friend who is faithful and kind, or wanting God to intervene and change the situation.

After that, we can begin to help our children see how to participate in what God does. The Israelites had to pick up the manna in the morning and make it into bread. God may bring an opening of provision, such as a new person at school, but it will be up to us to participate in his provision and go and make friends with that person. Night-time is a wonderful time to talk about our needs and worries, to bring them to God and discuss how we will respond when he provides.

4

A voice in the night

1 Samuel 3

Samuel shuffled through the dark night, back to his bed in God's house. He crumpled down on to his mat and curled his body back up into a ball. He was so tired. Every time he was almost falling asleep, he thought he heard Eli the priest call for him. Eli was old and couldn't see very well and often needed help, even in the middle of the night.

Twice he had got out of bed to go and see what Eli wanted. Twice Eli had looked at him confused and insisted he go back to bed. What was going on? He didn't think anyone would play tricks on him. Besides, no one else was around.

Samuel turned over and gazed at the seven flames flickering in God's lamp. He loved sleeping here. No place was more beautiful and peaceful than God's house at night. It was amazing to think that God himself was so close. His heavy eyelids began to close and the quiet sounds of the house began to fade away as he slowly drifted back to sleep. All was silent.

'Samuel!'

His eyes snapped open at the sound of his name. He tossed his rough blanket back and stumbled quickly to Eli's room once again. The night air was heavy and cold and he shivered a bit. Once he'd reached Eli's room, he took a small step inside and stopped. 'Here I am,' he whispered out to Eli in the darkness.

The room was quiet, yet Samuel could hear the faint sound of Eli rustling his blankets back and forth in his bed.

Samuel stepped close to the bed and gently shook Eli's shoulder. 'Here I am, Eli. You called me?'

Eli sighed deeply and mumbled, 'For the third time, I did not…' But then Eli stopped talking. And for a few moments he even stopped moving.

Samuel wasn't sure what to do. He bent down and looked closely at Eli's face. The old priest's eyes were closed but his eyebrows were squeezed together as if he were thinking very hard.

Soon Eli opened his eyes and slowly, carefully sat himself up. Then he looked straight into Samuel's eyes.

Even in the dim light, Samuel could feel that Eli was going to say something important. What was going on? What could possibly be happening that would make Eli look at him like this?

'Go to bed,' said Eli. 'If he calls you again, say, "Speak, Lord. I am your servant and I am listening."' Eli's crackly voice was clear this time, and it made Samuel's heart thump in his chest. Eli squeezed Samuel's shoulders and gave him a small nudge towards the door.

'Speak, Lord? As in… Lord God?' thought Samuel. 'It was God who was calling me? God of the universe, all-loving, all-powerful God? Calling me? In the middle of the night when no one was around?' Samuel's feet sped up and he raced back to his room, which was still lit with the gentle glow from the tiny flames of God's lamp. He froze in the room, looking around for… what? What did he expect? Samuel remembered that Eli had said he should lie back down, so he tiptoed to his little mat on the floor and lay down with his face towards the floor.

He waited.

And waited.

Then suddenly Samuel felt something. It was like warm chills on his back. He could feel that someone was standing in the room with him. And then the voice that had become so familiar to him spoke again.

'Samuel! Samuel!'

He couldn't tell whether he was hearing the voice with his ears or in his mind, but he knew that the voice was real. And now he knew whose voice it was. God's. Samuel kept his forehead firmly pressed into his pillow, and his heart jumped around inside his chest. He felt so small and blessed as he said out loud, 'Speak, Lord. I am your servant and I am listening.'

The quiet, steady voice of the Lord continued: 'Watch. I am going to do something in Israel…'

As Samuel listened with awe and wonder to the God who speaks in the night, he knew his life would never be the same again.

Extras for parents

Key truth: God communicates with us in the night.

Discussion

If you want to discuss this story with your children, here are some suggestions.

First, help your children recognise the key truth from the story. These questions will help you get started:

- Why did Samuel keep getting out of bed?
- Who was really talking to Samuel?
- The next time God called his name, how did Samuel respond?

You may want to continue the discussion and broaden your children's understanding of the story's key truth. Choose one or two of these questions to launch a conversation and see where it goes:

- Why didn't Samuel recognise that it was God calling him?
- Why do you think God chose the night-time to speak to Samuel?
- Why didn't God give up trying to talk to Samuel and find someone else instead?
- Have you ever felt God communicating with you at night? What was it like? Share how God communicates with you and how you are learning to recognise his communications. If you are at the beginning of this journey, feel free to share that too.

Pray

If you want to pray with your children, here is a prayer that may serve as a starting point.

Father God, thank you that you communicate with us at night. We don't want to miss anything you have to say to us, so we say to you tonight, 'Speak, God. We are listening.' Make all our nights full of chats back and forth with you. Thank you, God.

If you want to help your children connect with God and continue chatting with him on their own, here is one example for you.

Talk briefly with your children about how God communicated in many different ways with people in the Bible. Sometimes he used pictures, words or emotions to communicate his message. Our whole body is designed to catch God's communications.

Suggest that your children lie down, get comfortable and say to God in their minds or as a whisper, just like Samuel did, 'Speak, God. I am ready to listen with my whole body.'

Then leave lots of quiet space while you wait with God—at least 30 seconds, but longer if it feels right. Don't forget to let yourself be open to God's communication.

Check in with your children with open-ended questions: 'How are you feeling? What was God doing?' Share your story too.

'Parenting for faith' tool

Catching God's communication is important in our lives. All of us, children and adults, long to have that connection with God, to know his encouragement, his guidance and his truth in our lives. Night-time is a beautiful and natural setting for us to pursue communication with God. We are all on a journey of recognising God's communications more and more. Wherever you are on your journey, you are able to help your children step into their journey too.

If you want to know more about the biblical foundations behind this and how to do it well, you may want to read *Parenting Children for a Life of Faith* (BRF, 2010), which includes a number of chapters on helping children to catch God's communications.

5

Songs in the night

Psalm 88

with Psalms 33, 40 and 42; 1 Chronicles 6 and 15—16;
2 Chronicles 5

Heman squeezed his eyes shut and turned over on his
bed again. He had tossed back and forth for what seemed
like hours, trapped in the same thoughts. He couldn't find
sleep. He couldn't find peace. His heart hurt so much, he
thought he would never get to sleep ever again.

'Oh, God, I'm so sad,' Heman whispered. He lay on his back,
looking at the black ceiling, tears dripping down his face
and soaking his pillow. 'I have no friends any more, God. My
best friends hate me now. It's like everything's going wrong,
and I don't know how to fix it.' His words stopped as he
began to sob. It seemed that every time he thought about
his friends' disapproving looks or remembered their mean
words, he became sadder and sadder.

Heman turned on to his belly and buried his face in his
pillow. Why couldn't it all stop? Night-time is so hard when
you're sad. You're just trapped in the dark and quiet with
yourself. He remembered the story his grandfather Samuel
used to tell him, about when he had first heard God's voice.
Samuel said it had happened when he was a child, long
ago, while he was lying on his bed in God's house. Night-
time with God had been special in his family. He wished it
could be that way for him too, but now he just felt far away
from everyone, including God. Alone.

Then, unexpectedly, a familiar song quietly interrupted
his memories—a God song, a worship song. He had sung
it many, many times in his life. It was a simple song:

'Give thanks to the Lord, for he is good. His love lasts for ever.' He tried to push the song out of his mind. It was distracting him, and he was busy being sad, but it wouldn't go away. Heman began to get frustrated. He couldn't get comfortable, and now he had a song running around his head. He sat up and punched his pillow back into shape and flopped back down. Nothing seemed to work.

The song became stronger. He remembered the first time he had sung it. It was when he'd played the cymbals for God in the parade that had led God's ark up to the city of Jerusalem, where God's new home would be built. Oh, there was such excitement! Such happiness! A little smile flickered as Heman remembered all the good feelings of that day of celebration with God's people.

Heman curled up, wrapping his feet around the blanket, and began to speak to God in his thoughts: 'Remember how every day I would play you music and sing your praises while I was with you in your new home? I felt so special to be chosen to spend every day with you, thanking you for your love. Remember how you would whisper to me and show me wonderful things and give me messages for the king? I loved singing to you. I loved how close we were when I would sing and play you songs.'

Then Heman felt God moving close, like a cool breeze. He began to hum the tune that continued to play in his head, and he felt God's love fall over him like a blanket.

Heman began to sing the words in his mind. Every time he repeated them, he felt as if the chains of deep sadness were falling off his heart.

Then he began to sing the song out loud. 'Give thanks to the Lord, for he is good. His love lasts for ever.'

Happy tears began to wet his face as he sang alone to God in the middle of the night. He realised that, whether he was sad or happy, God still loved him very much. And whether things were going right or going wrong, God was still faithful as his friend. He was *not* alone. Heman wiped his tears and sang and sang, and, as he did, his heart lightened. Heman was so grateful that he served a God who brought him songs in the night.

Extras for parents

Key truth: God's songs connect us to him in the night.

Discussion

If you want to discuss this story with your children, here are some suggestions.

First, help your children recognise the key truth from the story. These questions will help you get started:

- What was Heman feeling at the beginning of the story? Why?
- What did God do that helped Heman remember his times with God?
- How did Heman feel after singing to God?

You may want to continue the discussion and broaden your children's understanding of the story's key truth. Choose one or two of these questions to launch a conversation and see where it goes:

- Why do you think God reminded Heman of a song instead of talking to him with words?
- Why do people feel close to God when they sing songs to him?
- What is your favourite worship song and why?
- Have you ever sung to God and experienced it changing your heart? Share a story of when you sang a song to God, and how it changed the way you felt about a situation. Invite your children to share their stories.

Pray

If you want to pray with your children, here is a prayer that may serve as a starting point.

Father God, thank you that when we are sad like Heman, you are there for us. Thank you for creating music. Tonight, as we lie on our beds in the night, remind us of songs to sing so that our hearts can connect with you in the dark. Thank you, God.

If you want to help your children connect with God and continue chatting with him on their own, here are a few suggestions:

- Offer to let them choose a worship CD to listen to as they go to sleep.
- Create a list of their favourite worship songs for them to keep in their rooms and use whenever they want, even in the middle of the night.
- Ask God to remind you of a worship song right now, and wait for 30 seconds. Whoever feels a song jump into their mind can start singing it to God out loud. If you know it, join in. When that song is done, wait in the quietness until someone else in your family starts singing one.
- Tell your children that Heman wrote a song when he was sad, and it's in the Bible—Psalm 88. King David often wrote songs to God in

the night. Let your children know that they can always make up new songs to sing to God too. That's how all of our worship songs are made. People connect with God and write songs to express themselves. Some songs are even written in the night.

'Parenting for faith' tool

Music is a powerful gift from God, and scripture is full of times when God's people used it in the night to praise, celebrate and draw close to God. Music can often unlock our emotions and help us connect with God. It can also create an atmosphere of thinking about God and creating space for him in the dark. During the night, what does your child need to be reminded of about God? It may be worth creating some space for worship songs to act as reminders of God's truth in the darkness, either by singing together or by providing music to listen to.

6

Awake all night

Daniel 6

with Psalm 121

Daniel held on tightly to the rope that was slowly lowering him into the dark pit. His heart was thumping with fear. Below him rumbled the deep growls of hungry lions.

'Daniel!' The king's terrified voice echoed down to him. 'Daniel! May your God rescue you!'

Daniel's feet hit the ground and he let go of the rope. He heard the scraping of a large rock being pushed across the entrance of the den, taking away the only escape route he had. He knew he was totally alone now. It would be just him and the lions.

Daniel squinted into the darkness, but it was hard for him to see anything clearly. He could hear the lions somewhere out in front of him, panting, grrrr-ing, and scratching their heavy claws against the hard ground. And then he heard the same sounds behind him, too. 'They're all around me!' he thought.

Death by lions. That's what the law said. He was here until the lions killed him. It was his punishment for talking with the God he loved.

'How can I even fight them? Why haven't they attacked yet?' As Daniel slowly turned around, his eyes caught sight of one lion staring straight at him, crouched low and ready to pounce.

'God, God… oh, God…' whispered Daniel, unable to think more words than his heart's cry for help. He heard a growl, and then a sudden swoosh of air blew past his face. He closed his eyes tightly and let out a terrified scream. His arms jerked up to protect his face from the lion's claws. Then he felt… nothing. No pain. No claws.

Daniel started to tremble. His mind raced with questions. Am I dead? What happened?

He opened his eyes and saw the most frightening, glorious sight of his life. In front of him stood a mighty angel of the living God, gripping the mouth of the lion that had pounced towards him. Daniel fell to his knees, shaking, and then he gazed in wonder as the angel moved quickly from one lion to the next, shutting each of their mouths tight. It was a magnificent sight.

Daniel watched until the angel had finished his work. Then he stumbled to the side of the den and rested his head against the rough cool wall. The lions were lying down now, all of them with their mouths shut.

Daniel sat in the darkness all night and talked with God. His heart was filled with deep thankfulness, and he felt wrapped in the love of his God. As Daniel drifted in and out of sleep and prayer, a memory of a God-poem floated in his mind. It was a poem from many hundreds of years before, written by another man who knew what it was like to live in danger.

Daniel whispered the words, 'I look up to the mountains; does my strength come from mountains? No, my strength comes from God, who made heaven, and earth, and mountains. He won't let you stumble, your Guardian God won't fall asleep… God guards you from every evil, he guards your very life. He guards you when you leave and when you return, he guards you now, he guards you always.'

Hours later, Daniel heard the patter of running footsteps and heard the desperate voice of the king yelling as soldiers began to pull back the rock guarding the entrance to the den.

'Daniel!' shouted the king. 'Servant of the living God, has your God saved you from the lions?'

The early morning light spilled softly into the lions' den. Daniel smiled and stood up, ready to tell the king about the power of his God, who never sleeps and is faithful and powerful to protect his people through the night.

Extras for parents

Key truth: God guards us at night.

Discussion

If you want to discuss this story with your children, here are some suggestions.

First, help your children recognise the key truth from the story. These questions will help you get started:

- Where did the king put Daniel as a punishment?

- What was supposed to happen to him in the lions' den?
- What did God do?

You may want to continue the discussion and broaden your children's understanding of the story's key truth. Choose one or two of these questions to launch a conversation and see where it goes:

- How do you think Daniel felt in the dark, at night, at the bottom of the lions' den? Do you ever feel that way at night?
- Why do you think God sometimes sends angels instead of rescuing people himself?
- Have you ever been in real danger, and God rescued you? Tell a story of when you were in danger and you felt that God intervened. Talk about how you felt, and invite your children to share stories of their experiences.

Pray

If you want to pray with your children, here is a prayer that may serve as a starting point.

Father God, thank you that you are our guardian. Thank you for being more powerful than anything that could ever put us in danger. Thank you for staying awake all night, never sleeping. Please stand guard over me tonight. Thank you, God.

If you want to help your children connect with God and continue chatting with him on their own, here are a few suggestions.

- Suggest that your children tell God what makes them afraid in the dark or the night. Then, after 30 seconds of quiet time, suggest that they ask God to come and be their guard all night, because he is more powerful than anything.

- Let your children ask God to remind them of a time when they were in danger and he guarded and rescued them. After some quiet time, ask them to share their stories with each other.
- Think about other people you know who need God's guarding, whether close or far away, and ask God to guard them from the danger that is in their life.

'Parenting for faith' tool

Sometimes we shy away from talking about God as our guardian at night because we are afraid of the 'But what about…?' questions that can arise. Some of us adults may have had terrible things happen in our lives at night, and some children may not have always been safe at night, either. Difficult situations bring about tough questions, but parenting children for faith is about letting all the tough questions exist, and not being afraid of them. Night-times are often filled with all kinds of tough questions, and some are about God: 'How can he be real when I can't see him? Did he really make the earth in seven days?'

A key skill to learn is how to have a conversation about the tough questions. I suggest the following four-step pattern:

1. What do you think?
2. What do we know from the Bible and from wise people?
3. How does it affect my relationship with God?
4. Share a bit about how you personally deal with the question in your life.

As an example, if a child asked, 'How do I know that God is real when I can't see him?' you could continue the conversation by using this pattern.

1. What do you think? [Listen…] That's really interesting.
2. Well, we know that God is very real. I know because I talk with him, and I see him doing wonderful things in my life. I read in the Bible that people throughout history have known him and seen him do things. But you are also right—I can't see him in the same way that I see you.
3. I think it's like when I'm talking to Grandma on the phone. She is very real, I can hear her, and she has a great impact on my life. But when I'm on the phone, I can't see her. Or it's like the wind. I see the wind, I feel it, I'm amazed at how it shakes the trees, but I can't see the wind itself. I sometimes wish I could see God, but I'm learning every day how to be connected to him even when my eyes can't see him.
4. How do you feel about that?

If your child asks a tough question that you can't answer, feel free to say, 'I don't know. Let's find out together.' Make a plan to ask your church leader or a wise friend, or set aside time to look it up in the Bible together. Enjoy your child's curiosity about the things of God. It is one of the great and wonderful privileges we have—wading into the tough questions with our children, with no fear.

7

No ordinary night

Matthew 2

with Numbers 24 and Daniel 9

The sands of the desert spread out as far as an ocean and surrounded the tower at the edge of the city. Farid stood motionless on the tower's flat roof, looking up at the moonless black sky.

'What *is* that?' Farid murmured to himself. He squinted again into the vast darkness speckled with tiny points of starlight. 'Hey, Ata!' he called out towards the staircase.

'What?' a faraway voice yelled up.

'Come here. I want you to look at this!' Farid fumbled with the star charts laid out on a small table next to him, examining one, then comparing it to another. He couldn't find what he was looking for on any of them.

The thumping of his friend's footsteps got closer, and Ata finally popped up from the staircase. 'What's up?'

Farid steered his friend to the short wall at the edge of the roof and pointed to a spot in the sky. 'Look at that bright star. Right there. Have you seen it before? Am I going crazy? That isn't supposed to be there. Right?'

Ata tilted his head to one side and focused hard on the bright star just above the horizon. 'No. It's… not supposed to be there.'

Farid turned toward his friend. 'What does it mean?'

Ata didn't answer. He just continued to stare at the little gem twinkling. Finally, he said quietly, 'It couldn't possibly be… unless…' He stopped talking and shook his head. He turned to Farid. 'OK. First of all, let's add this star to our records. Record the date and time when you first saw it. It's important.'

Farid looked through all the charts scattered on the table, found the day's log, and scratched in the details. Farid couldn't believe they were the first to find this new star. The others were going to be so excited to hear about this discovery. Then a flicker of memory poked his mind. What had Ata started to say? Hmmm. 'Hey, Ata, what did you mean when you said, "It couldn't possibly be…"?'

Ata's hand tightened on the scroll he was holding. 'My grandma used to tell me a story from her people about a new king, anointed by God, who would conquer kingdoms and save everybody. She said we would know he was here when a new star rose in the sky.'

Farid held his breath for a second. 'People were talking about this new star over 40 years ago?'

'No, not 40 years ago.' Ata gulped. 'My grandma said a man named Balaam spoke that message from the God of Israel over a *thousand* years ago. What are the chances that Balaam meant our own time… now?' Ata looked down at the scroll in his hands, and then his eyes widened. 'Hey, wait a minute,' he said. 'I have an idea. I'll be back in a second.' He dropped the scroll on the table and ran down the stairs.

Farid could hear him clunking around below in the library, bumping past shelves and ruffling through scrolls.

'Got it!' Ata yelled as he thundered back up to the roof. 'I read this ages ago. It's another prophecy, from another time when someone heard something from God about the future. It's 450 years old. This prophecy has loads of numbers to help you work out when the new king is supposed to come. Let me see.'

Ata opened the scroll and examined it, up and down and left and right, looking for the particular prophecy he had remembered reading before. 'There it is!' He picked up his quill and started scratching down numbers from the prophecy, murmuring as he did the maths. Finally, Ata put down his quill and stared at Farid.

'Well, what did you find?' Farid cried out.

Ata's eyes widened. 'According to my maths, the star to signal a new king could be any time now. Maybe this is it.'

The men turned and looked up at the bright star glowing in the distant sky, exactly where it was supposed to be.

Farid stood in wonder, thinking about the prophecies, thinking about a God who could use the night sky as his noticeboard. 'Ata,' he said softly, 'who *is* this God who tells people, hundreds and hundreds of years ahead of time, what will happen? And what must this new king be like?'

Ata smiled. 'We've got to go and see this king that the world has been looking for, for over a thousand years. We do not want to miss this.'

Extras for parents

Key truth: God knows the future and nothing
is too big for him to do.

Discussion

If you want to discuss this story with your children, here are some suggestions.

First, help your children recognise the key truth from the story. These questions will help you get started:

- What were Farid and Ata looking at in the sky?
- Ata remembered that God had promised something a long time ago. What had he promised?
- What had God said the new star would mean?
- Can you guess what happens next in the story?

You may want to continue the discussion and broaden your children's understanding of the story's key truth. Choose one or two of these questions to launch a conversation and see where it goes:

- Why do you think God wanted to tell people about something, hundreds of years before he did it?
- Why do you think God chose to tell people about his Son, Jesus, during the night?
- The wise men struggled to understand how big and powerful and mysterious God is. What are the things you still don't understand about God or the world?

Pray

If you want to pray with your children, here is a prayer that may serve as a starting point.

Father God, you are so different from us! You are so big, and you know all the things that are going to happen in the future—tomorrow and in hundreds and thousands of years. Thank you for knowing all our tomorrows, and for still loving us tonight. We can't understand all of you, God, and that is OK. You are God, and we are happy to be with you. Thank you, God.

If you want to help your children connect with God and continue chatting with him on their own, here are a few suggestions:

- Suggest that they spend time chatting with God about something they don't understand about him or the world. Read to them Jeremiah 33:3: 'Call to me and I will answer you and tell you great and unsearchable things you do not know' (NIV). Encourage them to keep close to God as they chat with him.
- Give your children a choice of books with pictures of our galaxy, and encourage them to look through it with God and chat with him about how amazing his creation of stars and planets is.

'Parenting for faith' tool

God is unfathomable. He is beyond our understanding. We can often feel pressure to have all the answers, particularly at night-time, but it is actually healthy for us to say, 'I wonder about that too.' If we always have an explanation for God, we are giving our children a small view of him. Feel free to wonder aloud and say, 'You know what amazes me?

God knows what job I'm going to have 30 years from now! Isn't that crazy? Wow!'

Allow the wonder of our astonishing God to flow out of you, and your children will learn to let it flow out of them, too.

8

Overnight chat

Matthew 14

with Mark 1; Luke 5—6

The waves slapped gently against Andrew's boat as it lay anchored just off shore on the Lake of Galilee. Andrew sat in the boat, coiling rope as the night began to creep across the sky. Jesus had seemed keen for them to get going quickly, so Andrew had hurried ahead to ready his boat. The cool evening breeze was picking up now. It felt good.

Andrew coiled another length of rope and scanned the shoreline, looking for his fellow disciples. He hoped they'd be along any minute. His tired eyes managed to locate his friends. They were weaving their way down the hillside, through the crowd of people and towards the shore.

'Woooo hoo!' one friend shouted as he splashed his way through the shallow water and threw himself over the side into the boat. 'That was amazing. There must have been thousands and thousands of people there. And Jesus fed them all. All!'

'I know!' Andrew grinned at his friend's excitement. 'Jesus constantly surprises me.' He waved to the rest of the disciples, who were now sloshing through the water towards him. The boat gently rocked as the disciples piled in.

Andrew squinted through the dim light and saw his brother, Peter, on shore chatting with Jesus. Jesus smiled and said something that made Peter laugh. Then Jesus patted Peter on the shoulder and began walking back up the hill towards the people. Peter quickly turned towards Andrew and gave the signal to start pulling up the anchor.

'Isn't Jesus coming?' called Andrew. He raised his eyebrow quizzically at Peter as he waded through the water and climbed in.

'No,' said Peter. 'Jesus wants us to go ahead of him across the lake while he sends everyone home. I think he's planning to spend some time alone with God tonight. You know, one of his overnight chats.'

Andrew nodded. 'He seems to love spending time alone at night with God.' Andrew secured the anchor, and the boat began drifting away from shore. He turned to Peter. 'Do you remember the first time we were with Jesus when he went away for an overnight chat?' Andrew's smile grew large.

'I do!' burst out Peter. 'We didn't know what had happened to him. It nearly scared us to death!' Peter leaned back and started laughing.

'What? Why have we never heard this story?' asked Philip, one of the disciples in the back of the boat.

'That's right—I forgot there were only four of us then.' Peter wrapped the sail's rope around his wrist and began.

'It was a night when we were at my mother-in-law's house, and Jesus had healed her of a fever that day. Once people heard Jesus was there, the whole town came by, and Jesus healed many of them too. We were exhausted and slept really deeply that night. But Andrew woke up in the middle of the night for some reason and noticed that Jesus was gone. Gone!'

'I was so confused!' Andrew chuckled. 'We were supposed to be his followers, and I didn't know where he was or where he would go in the middle of the night. None of us knew about the chats, yet.'

Peter adjusted the sail. 'Andrew woke us all up and we went searching for Jesus. We didn't want to get left behind. There we were, wandering up and down the streets, barely awake, trying to find the man we were supposed to be following.'

All the disciples started laughing, picturing everyone being so confused.

Peter continued. 'Of course, we finally found Jesus, and he told us he had left the house because he wanted to find a place to spend time with God, alone. Then he said, "Let's go to the nearby villages so that I can preach there as well. That is why I've come." And… off we went!'

The breeze picked up, and the boat began to bounce against the waves.

'So does Jesus do that a lot?' asked Phillip.

Andrew nodded. 'I'm noticing it more and more. Remember the day he chose us twelve as apostles? He'd spent the night before on a mountainside with God. There's something special, I think, about a night alone with God, just talking heart to heart. Jesus always comes back changed, stronger, more sure of what to do. Sometimes he comes back and does something new and radical and full of power. A night alone with God is… something wonderful for Jesus.'

Philip stared at the waves sparkling in the moonlight. 'Andrew… have you ever spent a night alone with God?'

'No… not yet, Philip.' He sighed. 'Maybe I should.'

Peter looked back towards the shrinking shore. 'I wonder how Jesus is going to catch up with us.'

Andrew smiled gently. 'After a night with God? I'm sure he'll come up with something.'

Extras for parents

Key truth: God loves to chat with us in the night.

Discussion

If you want to discuss this story with your children, here are some suggestions.

First, help your children recognise the key truth from the story. These questions will help you get started:

- Why didn't Jesus go in the boat with the disciples?
- Were there other times when Jesus chose to go on an overnight chat with God? Tell me about them.
- Can you guess what happened next? How did Jesus catch up with them in the boat?

You may want to continue the discussion and broaden your children's understanding of the story's key truth. Choose one or two of these questions to launch a conversation and see where it goes:

- Why do you think Jesus liked chatting with God in the night? What is different about the night-time, that Jesus may have liked?
- Why do you think God likes chatting with us?
- When is your favourite time to chat with God, and why?
- Is there anything you can't chat with God about? Why?

Pray

If you want to pray with your children, here is a prayer that may serve as a starting point.

Father God, thank you that you love to chat with us at night. Thank you for this special time of quiet and peace when we can share about our days and talk about anything. Thank you, God.

If you want to help your children connect with God and continue chatting with him on their own, here are a few suggestions. It works best if you make the suggestion and then they chat with God in their minds or whisper into their hands so that you don't hear. Either way, after you've made the suggestion, pause for at least 30 seconds of quiet time to allow your children to connect with God on their own.

Tell God:

- your favourite place to be in the world
- the person you want to be friends with for ever
- one thing you wish was different about your family
- a joke
- an adult you would like to be like when you grow up
- a story in the Bible that you wish you could have seen in real life
- one thing you hope God would do for your mum or dad
- one person at school who makes you feel small
- something you want to be able to learn super-fast
- your favourite time you have ever had with God

'Parenting for faith' tool

Children love chatting with God at night. One girl described it as having a 'sleepover with God'. As parents, we can sometimes get tied up in attempts to give our children a formula for prayer, when they actually need to be released to share their whole hearts and minds with him. Create opportunities for them to chat with God while you're not listening. As you leave their room, say, 'I love you. Have a nice chat with God!' to remind them that although you are leaving, God is still with them and ready to listen. Allowing our children to spend their nights chatting with God sets them up for a lifetime of nights with him.

9

Rescue in the dark

Acts 12

Rhoda forced open her tired eyes and straightened her slumped body. She couldn't believe she had let herself fall asleep. Was it time for the sun to come up yet? It felt so very late. Inside the little home, the light from one small candle barely lit the faces of the men and women around her who were softly praying together.

The last few days had been so sad and frightening. Jesus' friend Peter had been arrested and was probably going to be killed. Since no one knew what to do to help Peter, his friends had decided to get together to do the most powerful thing they could think of—ask God to help and keep praying until something happened.

Rhoda had often listened to Peter speaking about Jesus, the Son of God. Her life had now become so full of light and joy. She knew that if God could rescue her from sin, he could certainly rescue Peter from a cold, awful prison. She clenched her fist with determination and went back to praying. 'You are a big God. Please help Peter.'

On the other side of the room, a man wiped away tears and prayed, 'Oh, God of the universe, king of all, set our friend Peter free! Rescue him, God!'

Rhoda nodded her head in agreement and joined him and the others in prayer.

'Yes, God. Peter needs a miracle! Rescue him!'

The prayers and soft cries grew louder and louder and filled the dim little room. A fire of emotions leapt up in Rhoda's heart, and tears flooded her eyes. Just last week, King

Herod had killed another one of Jesus' disciples, James. It felt as if, at any moment, any one of them could be taken and thrown into prison, or worse. She took a deep breath. She couldn't imagine how Peter felt, held by chains, not knowing what would happen next. Her heart returned to determined prayer.

Just then, Rhoda thought she heard several knocks on the front door. She looked around the room to see if anyone else had heard it.

The knocks came again, faster and louder. This time, everyone stopped praying and listened.

'I'll go and see who it is,' Rhoda said, cautiously. She slowly rose to her feet and made her way through the crowd. She pressed her ear against the locked door. 'H-hello? Who's out there?'

'Rhoda, is that you?' whispered the voice. 'It's me, Peter! Please open the door.'

Rhoda gasped and then stumbled back a few steps. It *was* Peter's voice. But… how could it be him? A spark of joy began deep inside Rhoda and rushed through her body like lightning. She spun around and ran at full speed to the back room, to her waiting friends. 'It's Peter!' she exclaimed. 'Peter's at the door!'

The men and women stared back at her, seeming confused. 'You're out of your mind,' one young man said.

The knocks began again. This time they didn't stop.

The young man scrambled to his feet, headed straight for the door, and quickly unlocked it. The others ran after him, crowding around the opening to see who was standing in the darkness.

Looking back at them was the smiling face of their friend Peter. In a swell of excitement, everyone, including Rhoda, broke out in cheers and hugs and deep thanks to God.

After a minute, Peter waved his hands to quieten them.

'Well, what happened, Peter?' Rhoda asked. 'How did you escape from prison? Tell us!'

Peter smiled. 'I was sleeping between two soldiers, all chained up, and then I felt a poke in my side. I opened my eyes and saw an angel telling me to put on my shoes and clothes and cloak and follow him. My chains just fell off my wrists. They just fell off! I followed the angel and we walked past guards and through gates that opened all by themselves. I thought God was showing me something in a dream. I wasn't sure it was real at all. Then, when I was on the street, the angel just disappeared.'

Peter paused and a stillness spread through the little community of people as they became aware of the amazing wonder of God's love and power.

Rhoda looked at all the shining faces around her, wet with happy tears. She was so grateful that she served a God who would listen to their prayers in the middle of the night and rescue their friend who was sleeping in prison.

Extras for parents

Key truth: God is at work, rescuing and doing great things in the night.

Discussion

If you want to discuss this story with your children, here are some suggestions.

First, help your children recognise the key truth from the story. These questions will help you get started:

- Why were the people in the house worried about Peter?
- What were they doing to help Peter?
- What was God doing while they were praying?

You may want to continue the discussion and broaden your children's understanding of the story's key truth. Choose one or two of these questions to launch a conversation and see where it goes:

- Why do you think Rhoda was so surprised to see Peter at the door when she had been praying all night for him to be rescued?
- Why do you think God didn't tell the praying people what he was doing at that exact moment?
- Has God ever rescued you? Or do you know any story of God rescuing other people?
- God is a rescuer. Who do you know who needs rescuing right now?

Pray

If you want to pray with your children, here is a prayer that may serve as a starting point.

Father God, you are the great action-God, doing wonderful rescues in the night. Thank you that you never stop to sleep, but you are working through the night. God, be the rescuer now! [Pray for anyone you know who needs rescuing, including any of your family members.] We look forward to waking up and seeing what you have been doing tonight. Thank you, God, our rescuer.

If you want to help your children connect with God and continue chatting with him on their own, here are a few suggestions.

- Ask your children to think of someone who needs rescuing. It may be one of them or someone else. Invite them to draw a picture of the person and, as they draw, to chat to God about the situation and what the person needs. Put the picture of the person on their wall by their bed, so that whenever they look at it they can remember to chat quickly to God about that person.
- For older children, grab a newspaper that you are comfortable with, and allow them to flip through a few pages and choose something that strikes their heart and makes them feel compassionate. Give them space to read a bit of the article, then encourage them to chat to God about it, asking him to rescue and fix the situation. As the days go by, keep an eye on that story to see what God is doing, and talk about it.

'Parenting for faith' tool

At bedtime, our children may have specific things they want to pray about—a friend who is ill, a test coming up, or a stressful happening at playgroup or school. Often, we pray about these things fervently and forget about them the next day. Nights are a perfect time for building up a child's faith, to know that when we pray, God is active and working on the situation in response to our prayers and his plans.

If this is particularly pertinent to your family at the moment, I suggest that you make a prayer journal—just a piece of paper or small book where you write down anything specific that is burdening your children. As you and they continue to pray for the situation, come back to the journal the next day or the next week and discuss with them what God has done. This way, your children will develop a nightly expectation of God's action while they sleep.

10

Hidden in the night

1 Samuel 23 and Psalm 139 (*THE MESSAGE*)
with Psalms 63, 73 and 130

The moonlight danced on the waterfall, bouncing shimmering light on to the stone walls of the canyon. David sat alone on a boulder, staring at the swirling reflections of stars in the river. He crinkled his forehead in frustration and twisted a stick over and over in his hand as his mind spun in thought.

It was all just so unfair. He had done nothing to deserve being treated like this. Nothing! King Saul had been chasing him for years, trying to kill him. Trying to kill him for doing all the right things. He'd obeyed the king, fought for the king and tried to help the king. But even after all that, the king was determined to hunt him down and kill him. It was so unfair! Would the king ever stop?

David dipped his hands in the cool, black river, scooped up some water and poured it over his head. The heat of the day still glowed from the rocks around. He couldn't sleep. No matter how hard he tried, he couldn't get his brain to turn off. Like the waterfall in front of him that would never stop flowing, his heart couldn't stop pouring out broken and angry thoughts and feelings. He was helpless—unable to change the king's actions. So he was stuck. He stood up and threw the crushed stick as far as he could into the water, and he watched it disappear.

Hiding. He was stuck hiding. Hiding in the dark. Hiding to save his life. Hiding all alone. He felt as if he had disappeared, just like that stick.

A light flashed across the water. Could it be a shooting star? David craned his head back to search the vast universe above. His eye caught another flash. There it was again. A smile spread across his face as he studied the skies above. God was so amazing to make all of that! Wait. David paused for a second as the whisper of God dropped a thought in his mind: 'You are hiding. Yes. But you could never be hidden from me.'

David leapt off the boulder and scrambled for his bag, pulling out something to write on. He was a fool. The sense of God's hand on his back relaxed his shoulders. His eyes began to sparkle. 'Hiding, but not hidden,' he said to himself.

Lit only by moonlight, David began to write: 'Is there any place I can go to avoid your Spirit? to be out of your sight? If I climb to the sky, you're there! If I go underground, you're there! If I flew on morning's wings to the far western horizon, you'd find me in a minute—you're already there waiting!'

David flung his head back, and happy tears filled his eyes. Yes, it *was* unfair. Yes, the king *was* threatening his life. But what was a man next to God? His heart leaped again and his pen returned to the paper: 'Oh, he even sees me in the dark! At night I'm immersed in the light! It's a fact: darkness isn't dark to you; night and day, darkness and light, they're all the same to you.'

David's anger was gone. His frustration had vanished. Everything looked so different now. Tomorrow would be another day. But tomorrow would be filled with peace, and tomorrow would be seen and guided by God.

Tonight, David would sleep—sleep with a quiet heart. Even though he was hidden from the eyes of men, he knew he would always be seen by God. He was held by the God who would never be far from him.

Extras for parents

Key truth: God can always see us. We are never hidden from him.

Discussion

If you want to discuss this story with your children, here are some suggestions.

First, help your children recognise the key truth from the story. These questions will help you get started:

- Why was David hiding?
- What was he feeling?
- Where was God while David was feeling all those things?
- What did God do?

You may want to continue the discussion and broaden your children's understanding of the story's key truth. Choose one or two of these questions to launch a conversation and see where it goes:

- Why do you think David felt so alone in the dark?
- How do you think God felt when he saw David feeling so angry and upset?

- Night-time can often make us feel hidden, as if no one sees us and we are alone. When David felt like that, he wrote to God. What do you do when you feel lonely? (As a parent, tell your story of what you do when you feel lonely. Invite your children to share their experiences, too.)
- Have you ever heard someone else's writing that helped you connect with God? Have you ever heard any of David's psalms?

Pray

If you want to pray with your children, here is a prayer that may serve as a starting point.

Father God, thank you that we are never truly alone because you can always see us. Sometimes we feel hidden from the world, all alone. When we feel like this, remind us that you are there next to us, in our hidden place. Thank you for loving us so much that you want to stay close to us. Thank you, God.

If you want to help your children connect with God and continue chatting with him on their own, here are some suggestions.

The psalms are full of people's writings to God or about God, and they are filled with many different emotions. Your children may want to write their own psalm about God—what he is like, what they are feeling, and what they want him to do with them. Perhaps each family member can find a place to go to write a psalm, out of their heart-connection with God. Some may want to share their psalm; others may not. Both are OK. If you have younger children, you can ask them questions and write their words down in psalm form.

Go on a little adventure to help your children connect with God through someone else's words. If you can, pick a night that is clear enough to see the stars. Wrap up warm and head outside. If this isn't possible, ask your children to close their eyes and imagine looking at the stars, or look at pictures of stars in a book or on a computer.

Whether you are outdoors or inside, while they are looking, ask them to listen to the words of Psalm 19:1–4 and remember that God is right there with them. Read the verses several times, pausing to be quiet between readings.

The heavens declare the glory of God,
and the skies announce what his hands have made.
Day after day they tell the story;
night after night they tell it again.
They have no speech or words;
they have no voice to be heard.
But their message goes out through all the world;
their words go everywhere on earth. (NCV)

Ask your children how they feel about God when they look at the stars, and what message they think the stars give them about God.

'Parenting for faith' tool

Creativity is a wonderful path for connecting with God at night. Sometimes we feel, as parents, that 'craft' is a daytime activity and at night we just want to do things that are calm and straightforward. For some children, though, their connection with God benefits from writing to him, listening to scripture, drawing him pictures, and so on.

Open opportunities for your children to experience being creative. If some of them enjoy it, help them take the next step in using their creativity to connect with God. Perhaps give them a notebook to keep by their bed to write and draw in, to use just for creative communication between them and God. Our goal is not to prescribe how they connect with God, but to facilitate whatever works best for them. For some, creativity in the night is priceless.

11

Sleeping in the storm

Acts 23 and 27

with Philippians 4:8 and Luke 8

Paul yawned slowly and tried to find a more comfortable way to sleep on his cot. He was now a prisoner, being held in the army barracks in Jerusalem. It was late at night and the soldiers had stopped walking around. Everything was quiet and still.

Paul took a deep breath, closed his eyes and tried to fall back asleep. But then he sensed that someone was standing near him. Paul froze, senses alert. Then, with a wave of recognition, he realised. This was God.

The more Paul spent time with God in prayer and doing things with him, the more Paul knew him. Many years ago, when he'd first met Jesus, Jesus had appeared to him in a blinding light to get his attention. But now, even with his eyes closed, Paul knew the very peaceful feeling of God standing close. He waited, aware of God's deep love and strength nearby.

'Take courage!'

God's voice went straight to Paul's mind and heart. He didn't know if he was hearing it with his ears, but the words were clear.

'You have told people about me here in Jerusalem, but now you must go and tell people about me in Rome.' Then, as quickly as he'd appeared, the sense of him was gone.

Paul lay still. Rome? Rome was far away, at the very centre of the empire. He thought about what an adventure that would be. What a great God he served, who would send him to Rome to speak about him. What wonderful plans God makes! With a faint smile on his face, Paul returned to sleep.

Two years later, in the very middle of the night, Paul stood on the deck of a ship heading for Rome. He was bracing himself against the side-rails, clinging on tightly so that he wouldn't be tossed overboard by the massive storm. His muscles shook with every effort. Cold, hard rain stung his cheeks. For over a week, black clouds had poured down thick, grey rain. Gusting winds shoved the ship sideways, and crushing, deep waves slammed into the side of the ship, tossing it about, over and over again.

The people on board were exhausted. They were out of food, out of safety gear, and out of hope.

Paul saw that his friend Luke was trying to shout something to him, but the noise of the storm drowned out the voice. Paul's eyes locked on to Luke's, and between them they understood each other. They were going to die. There was no hope of being saved. Paul pushed his forehead against the rough, cold, wet wood of the ship and squeezed his eyes shut. There was nothing but the dark, terrifying sea raging all around him.

Then, in a moment, something or someone was standing beside him. It was a familiar presence, but it wasn't quite God. It was his messenger, an angel, with the peace of God pulsing from him.

'Do not be afraid, Paul,' said the angel. 'You must stand trial before Caesar in Rome. Not only will God save your life so that you can do this, but he will also graciously save the lives of all the people on this boat.'

As the angel disappeared, Paul began to laugh. All those months ago, God had told him that he would be sent to Rome. Why had he doubted that? Why had he allowed this storm to seem more powerful than the promise of God? He opened his eyes and looked around at the raging wind and rain.

Paul remembered that Jesus had been with his disciples in a boat during a storm once, and Jesus had slept through it. His disciples had had to wake him up. Paul laughed again. Jesus had slept in a storm, confident in the purposes of God.

Now Paul was confident too. All fear dissolved from his heart. He crawled to Luke to tell him what God's angel had said. Then he braced his body on the floor of the boat, the storm still screaming around him—and, with the smile of a man confident in God's plans, he fell into a deep, peaceful sleep.

Extras for parents

> Key truth: God's peace can help us sleep in any situation.

Discussion

If you want to discuss this story with your children, here are some suggestions.

First, help your children recognise the key truth from the story. These questions will help you get started:

- What was Paul's assignment from God?
- How did Paul know that God was standing next to him in prison?
- During the storm, why did Paul and Luke think they were going to die?
- What made Paul peaceful enough to go to sleep?

You may want to continue the discussion and broaden your children's understanding of the story's key truth. Choose one or two of these questions to launch a conversation and see where it goes:

- Why would God let Paul be in a storm, instead of taking the storm away so that Paul wouldn't get scared?
- Sometimes it is hard to sleep when we feel as if our life is a storm. Why?
- Think about a time when you had a personal or family storm. How did you sleep and what did God do?
- Have you ever had something bad happen, which made it hard for you to sleep? What did you do? (As a parent, share a story of when you found it hard to sleep and what God did to help you sleep. Invite your children to share their stories and experiences.)

Pray

If you want to pray with your children, here is a prayer that may serve as a starting point.

Father God, sometimes we feel as if everything is going wrong and we are scared that it will all fall apart. Thank you that sometimes you just stop the storm. Thank you that sometimes you let the storm go on, but you bring us so much peace that we can sleep right in the middle of it.

Right now, please bring us your peace so that we can sleep deeply and well, no matter what has happened today. Thank you, God.

If you want to help your children connect with God and continue chatting with him on their own, here are a few suggestions:

Invite your children to have some time alone with God to tell him about the storms in their lives. Encourage them to ask God to remind them of his strength, peace and comfort in difficult times. A few Bible verses you can look at together are Psalm 9:9; Psalm 37:5; Psalm 46:1; Romans 8:28 and John 14:27.

Some children dwell on the storms in their lives, and that causes them anxiety and difficulty in sleeping. Paul wrote to the Philippians, 'Finally, brothers and sisters, whatever is true, whatever is noble, whatever is right, whatever is pure, whatever is lovely, whatever is admirable—if anything is excellent or praiseworthy—think about such things' (4:8, NIV).

Encourage your children to brainstorm examples of everything on the list in this verse, and to fall asleep talking to God about these things. You might need to brainstorm with the children until they get the hang of it. Alternatively, encourage them to draw pictures of some of the things on their list—lovely things, for instance—and chat with God about them. This pattern of connecting with God and disciplining our thoughts can be very powerful in breaking cycles of worry and anxiety at night.

'Parenting for faith' tool

Watching our children go through emotional or spiritual storms is heartbreaking as a parent. Our instinct is to protect them and try to calm the storm, but, as you already know, this isn't always possible. Storms will come to our children. God has placed us in our children's lives to coach them in how to weather the storms healthily and with peace, rather than trying to solve every storm. Your presence and wisdom in their lives will equip and encourage them as they learn to find God's peace in the midst of their storms.

12

More real than real

Genesis 28

Jacob scrambled up a steep part of the path, touching his hand to the ground for balance. He was so tired. These hills were always difficult to walk over, and he wasn't even sure he wanted to make the journey. Life just wasn't working out the way he wanted. He had messed up at home, and now his brother seriously wanted to kill him, so he was being sent away until it was safe. It all felt so pointless. Do this. Do that. Go here. Go there. He wished he had something important to do with his life, something more than just doing what his parents told him to do.

Jacob kicked a rock on the path and watched as it rolled down the side of the hill. He thought of his father, Isaac, and of his father's final prayer for him. His father had prayed that God would bless him. His father had also prayed that God would give him the same blessings that he'd promised to Jacob's grandfather, Abraham. It was a promise of land to live on, of a future for his family that would bless the whole world, and of a closeness with God himself. His father talked about it a lot—how God himself had chosen his family to do great and important things. Both his grandfather and his father believed it was true, but Jacob had never really met this God. He had just heard the stories. So what did those promises really have to do with him?

Darkness was settling on the land. Jacob looked back and watched the sun as it finished setting. He was tired. Bone tired. He dragged a stone to a fairly clear place on the ground and lay down, using the stone as a pillow. Not as comfortable as his bed at home, but it would do. Jacob watched the stars for a while and thought about his future. Then he closed his eyes, listened to the gentle breeze ruffling through the trees, and drifted into sleep.

He dreamed.

This dream was so bright, so clear, so different from all Jacob's normal dreams. This was a dream from God.

In his dream, Jacob saw a stairway. The first step was on the ground, and the rest of the steps went up and up, up and up, up and up into the sky, reaching all the way to heaven. Angels of God were busily going up and down the stairs, full of God's purposes. Above it all stood God, indescribable and holy.

Then God spoke to Jacob: 'I am God—the God your father and grandfather know. I am giving the ground that you are sleeping on to you and your children. Your growing family will be so big that it will spread all over the earth. Everyone all around the world will be blessed by you and your children, and your family will live on and on for years to come. I am with you and I will stay by your side, guarding and watching over you wherever you go.'

Jacob awoke, startled and shocked. He knew, without a doubt, that in this dream the God of the universe had just spoken to him. He remembered every part of it—how God looked, the smell of the air, the sound of the angels' feet. It was so real and perfect and bright and peaceful. It was so different from his usual dreams. This dream was more real than real.

The God who had spoken to his grandfather Abraham and to his father Isaac had now spoken to him, too. Here. Right here. While he slept. 'God is in this place, and I did not know it!' exclaimed Jacob. His heart fluttered as he looked at the place where, in his dream, the stairs from heaven had touched the ground. A gentle fear and wonder filled him as he began to understand that he had met God. 'This place is marvellous!' he exclaimed. 'God is here, right here. This place is like a gate to heaven.'

Alone on the side of the hill, Jacob sat in the quiet darkness, now aware of unseen angels all around and of the reality of God. He lay back down on the ground that God had promised to give him. God's words continued to echo in his head. His problems didn't seem to matter much at all now. The God who could speak in dreams had promised him wonderful things—a future and a hope, and, most of all, his closeness.

Jacob would never forget this night. He now knew who God was, and he knew that what God was doing was more real than anything he could see with his eyes.

Extras for parents

Key truth: God shows us more about himself
in dreams.

Discussion

If you want to discuss this story with your children, here are some suggestions.

First, help your children recognise the key truth from the story. These questions will help you get started:

- Why was Jacob upset in the beginning of the story?
- What did God show Jacob in his dream?
- How did Jacob feel different after he woke up from the dream?

You may want to continue the discussion and broaden your children's understanding of the story's key truth. Choose one or two of these questions to launch a conversation and see where it goes:

- Jacob had heard about God all his life, but he didn't know God personally. Why is hearing about God not enough to make us feel close to him?
- Why do you think God chose to talk to Jacob in his dream instead of when he was awake?
- Have you ever had a dream from God? How can you tell the difference? (As a parent, you could share a story of when you had a dream from God. Invite your children to share their stories and experiences, too.)

Pray

If you want to pray with your children, here is a prayer that may serve as a starting point.

Father God, thank you that you can talk to us even in our dreams. We want to learn more about you at all times. We are ready to meet you when we are awake and when we are asleep and dreaming. Please come close to us all night, and fill our dreams with thoughts of you. Thank you, God.

If you want to help your children connect with God and continue chatting with him on their own, here are a few suggestions:

- Encourage your children to invite God into their dreams, so that as they go to sleep, they will be aware that God is with them, even in their dreams.
- Encourage them to chat with God about their dreams and to tell him of any dreams that keep returning. They can ask God if he would change the stories in their returning dreams. What would they want the changes to look like?
- Give your children paper and pens to place by their bed, so that they can write down any dreams they want to talk about in the morning.

'Parenting for faith' tool

Children often feel quite powerless about their dreams. They can't control them, so they feel helpless about how to influence them. As parents, we know that we can't control their dreams, either, but the beautiful truth is that God is not powerless to intervene and help. Even though few of our dreams are from God, he does use dreams as one more way to communicate with his children.

We can model our trust in God's ability to be present in dreams. We can help our children to understand that there are no limits to where God can go. He can even meet them in their night-time dreams. As you pray for your children at night, feel free to build the anticipation of seeing God's goodness in their dreams. Invite God to be a part of their dreams, and ask him for his joy, love and adventure to be key parts of their dreams each night.

13

Gifts in the night

2 Chronicles 1 and 1 Kings 3

Solomon stood in the sunshine by the waters of Gihon. His stomach flip-flopped with excitement and fear. Against the hillside, people stood watching, shushing each other as they strained to listen. Solomon took a deep breath and closed his eyes. 'This is it,' he thought. 'There's no going back now.' The priest prayed and poured holy oil over Solomon's head, anointing him to be the next leader of the kingdom. The oil felt warm and smooth as it dripped through his hair and down his neck.

Then they blew the trumpet, and the people erupted in cheers and shouted, 'Long live King Solomon!' The joyful noise shook the ground, and it was wonderful and scary at the same time. It was official. Solomon was the prince who would become the next king. He hoped it would be a long time before he was left alone to run the kingdom.

But that wasn't to be. Only months later, his servant dashed into the garden breathing heavily. 'Come quickly, sir. Your father is dying and wishes to speak to you!'

Solomon's heart sank as he ran to his father's room and paused at the door.

'Come close, my son,' said King David, softly. A weak smile spread across his face.

Solomon sat next to him and held his thin, trembling hand.

'I am about to die like everyone else on earth,' said his father. 'So be strong and do what God asks of you. Obey everything he says, so that God will bless you in whatever you do and wherever you go.' His father sighed and drifted back to sleep. Solomon's throat tightened with sadness, almost choking him. Within a few hours, his father was dead.

Later, Solomon stood before the people with a crown on his head, hearing again the shouts of 'Long live King Solomon!' He looked out over the thousands in front of him—generals and judges, strong and powerful people. His heart pounded with fear. How could he lead these people? How could he ever know enough to be a good leader?

Only God knew. Only God. In an instant, his heart decided. Solomon raised his voice and shouted to the assembly, 'Join me! Let's all go and worship God together at his tent!'

And they went! Thousands walked together, dust billowing in clouds along the path. With every step, Solomon could feel the weight of being king sink deeper into his heart.

That night, after a day of worshipping God, Solomon crawled into bed, exhausted. Tomorrow he would have to start the everyday challenge of running a kingdom. 'I'm not ready,' he thought. He drifted off to sleep—and dreamed.

In the dream, God himself stood before Solomon and said, 'Ask for whatever you want me to give you.'

Solomon felt as if God could see all his secret thoughts and fears. 'God, my God, you have made me ruler of the kingdom in place of David my father. I'm too young for this. I feel like a child! I don't know how to do this job—how to be king of so many people, too many to even count. You asked me what I want. Please give me a wise heart and the knowledge I need so that I can lead your people. For who on their own is capable of leading your glorious people?'

In his dream, he could feel how pleased God was with his words. God spoke with love:

'Since your heart's desire is to have the wisdom and knowledge to lead, I will do what you have asked. Because you wanted this, and not money or long life or the death of your enemies, I will give you your heart's desire. I will give you a wise and discerning heart, so that there will never have been any king like you, nor will there ever be. And I will also give you what you didn't ask for. I will give you wealth and honour, and, if you walk in obedience to me, as your father David did, I will also give you a long life.'

And with one last touch of hearts, the dream was over.

Solomon sat up and stared in awe at the normal, grey walls of his tent. He was still the same person, king to numerous people. And yet, he felt different.

God had come to meet him in the night. God had given him this kingdom. And tonight, God had given him the gifts he needed to do the job he had been given. It was OK that he was young and new, because God's gifts were more powerful than Solomon's weaknesses.

Happy tears filled his eyes. His heart sang a new song of thanks for God's gifts in the night.

Extras for parents

Key truth: God gives gifts in the night.

Discussion

If you want to discuss this story with your children, here are some suggestions.

First, help your children recognise the key truth from the story. These questions will help you get started:

- Why was Solomon worried about being king?
- What did God agree to give Solomon in his dream?

You may want to continue the discussion and broaden your children's understanding of the story's key truth. Choose one or two of these questions to launch a conversation and see where it goes:

- Why do you think Solomon wanted to go and worship God when he felt overwhelmed? When Solomon worshipped God during the day, he didn't ask for anything. He just worshipped. Why?
- God was very pleased with Solomon's request for wisdom. Why did it make God so happy?
- God gave Solomon a big job, but Solomon didn't feel good enough to do it. Was that OK?
- What job has God given you? What more do you need from God to do it? (As a parent, you may want to share a story from your own experience.)

Pray

If you want to pray with your children, here is a prayer that may serve as a starting point.

Father God, thank you for your generous heart. You give such good gifts to us. Thank you that when you give us a big job, you don't leave us to fail; you give us everything we need. Tonight, as we rest and sleep, dream with us about big jobs you have for us to do. Thank you, God.

If you want to help your children connect with God and continue chatting with him on their own, here are a few suggestions.

- Encourage your children to spend some time just chatting with God about how wonderful he is, however they want to do that. Some may want to draw or write, while others may want to listen to a worship song. Solomon worshipped before he slept, and we can do that too.
- Suggest to your children that they ask God to look at all the bits of their heart. In Solomon's dream, God heard Solomon and was pleased with the desires in Solomon's heart. Our children can picture themselves showing all of their heart to God and having a chat with him about their desires, too.

'Parenting for faith' tool

As you know, sometimes we can't find the right words for what is going on in our hearts. At night, all of us feel the thoughts and emotions from the day beginning to surface. Time with God at night is wonderful because then we have a chance to process those thoughts and feelings with him. Our children sometimes need permission from us not to have to pray with words. Instead, they can spend some time relaxing with

God by simply saying, 'Here I am, God. Come and look at my mind and heart.'

In our story today, God responded to Solomon's heart's desires, and he is faithful to do so with our children tonight and every night. If you ever feel that words are blocking your child's connection with God at night, feel free to release them from that style of connection and open up new ways.

14

A clue to the future

Genesis 41

Pharaoh's eyes snapped open as he woke up once again. He knew he wasn't afraid. After all, his dark, cool bedroom in the palace was safe enough. But the memory of his dreams just wouldn't go away. They had been such silly dreams: seven skinny cows eating seven fat cows, and seven thin heads of grain swallowing seven healthy ones. Ridiculous.

Pharaoh flopped back on to his bed and tried to go back to sleep. Every time he closed his eyes, though, the same images of cows and grain kept appearing in his mind. They seemed to make no sense, yet he felt they were important somehow—as if he were supposed to understand something through them. But he just *didn't* understand.

The next day, Pharaoh, king of Egypt, asked his wise men for help, but no one could figure out his dreams. Finally, a servant told Pharaoh about a prisoner named Joseph who could interpret dreams, so Pharaoh called for Joseph to be brought to him.

Joseph was quickly taken out of the dungeon and came to Pharaoh.

Pharaoh raised an eyebrow as he studied this bony man walking in and standing before him. He waited a second and then spoke. 'I've heard it said of you that when you hear a dream you can interpret it.'

'I cannot do it,' said Joseph, 'but God will give Pharaoh the answer he desires.'

Pharaoh tilted his head to one side, took a deep breath, and told his dreams to the prisoner—every single detail.

Then there was a great silence in the room.

Finally, Joseph took a step forward and spoke, explaining to Pharaoh that the dreams of the cows and the grain meant the same thing. He continued, speaking quietly and firmly: 'God has shown Pharaoh what he is about to do. Seven good growing years are coming throughout the land of Egypt, but seven years of famine will follow them and will destroy the land. The reason the dream was given to Pharaoh in two different ways is that God has made up his mind, and it will happen soon.'

Pharaoh shook his head, trying hard to understand. Questions and worries filled his mind. 'What am I to do?' he asked himself. 'No country can survive seven years of famine.'

Famine meant that nothing would grow in the farms or fields. There would be nothing to eat. Famine meant that children would die. Famine meant cruelty in the streets as people became more and more desperate for food. Famine meant war as countries raided each other's lands to steal food. Famine meant death.

Joseph began to speak again, interrupting Pharaoh's thoughts. He suggested a plan to Pharaoh, a plan that would save his kingdom and save his people. But the plan would take work—seven years of hard work in the good times, in order to save enough food to eat in the seven bad years of famine.

Pharaoh looked around at his palace officials and then focused his eyes back on Joseph, the prisoner. 'Since God has spoken to you, I will trust you to be in charge of this plan to save us.'

Seven years later, Joseph and Pharaoh, king of Egypt, were ready. They stood on the palace balcony in the blazing heat and surveyed the long queue of people stretched before them.

Pharaoh leaned on the wall in wonder. The famine had come, just as God had said, and people were running out of food at home. Egyptians weren't the only ones who were hungry these days. Many other people across the region were without food. But the storehouses of Egypt were full, with enough food to feed the people through seven years of famine.

Pharaoh smiled. 'Joseph, my friend, the people have food today because you made us ready for this famine. Thank you.'

Joseph looked to the ground and said in a soft voice, 'Thank you for your kindness, Pharaoh, but we are ready because God was gracious enough to show you in a dream what he was about to do. We are ready because God was faithful enough to interrupt your sleep with a dream of the future. We are ready because of the living God.'

Pharaoh touched his friend on the shoulder. 'And I am grateful to him. Now let's open the storehouses and feed the people.'

Extras for parents

Key truth: God can prepare us for the future at night.

Discussion

If you want to discuss this story with your children, here are some suggestions.

First, help your children recognise the key truth from the story. These questions will help you get started:

- What was Pharaoh's dream about?
- What did Pharaoh and Joseph do for seven years to be ready for the famine?

You may want to continue the discussion and broaden your children's understanding of the story's key truth. Choose one or two of these questions to launch a conversation and see where it goes:

- Why do you think Pharaoh didn't just say, 'Oh, what a bad dream' and ignore it?
- Why would God send a dream to tell Pharaoh about something that was coming?
- Often we get worried about what will happen in the future, but God knows what will happen. How does that make you feel?

Pray

If you want to pray with your children, here is a prayer that may serve as a starting point.

Father God, thank you that you know what the future will bring. We feel safe in the knowledge that you see what is coming our way and know how to prepare us for it. As we sleep tonight and every night, continue to speak to us and prepare us for the future. Thank you, God.

If you want to help your children connect with God and continue chatting with him on their own, here are a few suggestions.

Invite your children to chat with God about the story, perhaps using some of the following approaches:

- Tell God what was the best part of the story.
- Tell God if you would rather be Pharaoh or Joseph in the story, and why.
- Tell God how you would feel if you had to live during a famine, a time when there was no food.
- Tell God one thing you hope he will do tonight with you in your dreams.

Chat a bit with your children about how no one but God knows the future. Encourage your children to feel free to talk with God about all their future hopes and to catch all of God's communications back about the wonderful tomorrows he has waiting for them.

'Parenting for faith' tool

Helping our children process their nights can be just as fruitful as helping them process their days. When they return home from school, we might ask them questions such as 'How was school? Was Gemma any kinder today? How did football go?' We deliberately seek to hear about their days and to understand how they feel about them.

Our children's nights are also meaningful times, and each morning we can help them process their experiences and feelings. This doesn't have to be a big event or take a long time. I suggest that a morning ritual of asking, 'How did you sleep? How was your night with God?' offers a brief opening for them to talk about their experience with God in the night-time. Some children will share more than others, and that's OK. Your daily understanding of their significant time with God each night will help you guide them into the next steps of their connection with him.

15

A change of heart

Matthew 1

Joseph stared at the little flame waving gently in the lamp on the table. The light created a warm, dim glow around him. His thoughts spun around in his head. What should he do? He'd never thought he would be in this situation. Never. Especially not with a woman like Mary.

Joseph dropped his head into his hands and rubbed his sore eyes. Was it possible for his soul to hurt? He had such an ache, deep inside. A few days ago he'd been a happily engaged man, so excited about his future, getting ready to marry a really good and godly woman. And now? Now he couldn't imagine being happy ever again.

Pregnant. Mary was pregnant. How? All he knew was that it was impossible for the baby to be his.

Joseph pushed his chair back and began to pace back and forth across the dimly lit room. Why had she done this? He felt so upset, so embarrassed. People would think they had broken God's law. What was he going to do?

Joseph dropped on to his bed and kicked his sandals across the room. It was so late. He hadn't slept much since Mary had told him about the baby. He curled under the covers and blew out the flame in the lamp. Pitch blackness filled the room.

He paused and just felt his heart beating for a while. He thought about all his choices—all the different things he could do now.

He could tell everyone that the baby wasn't his and it was all her fault. But… no. He couldn't leave her to be made fun of; he couldn't force people to notice her mistake.

He could accuse her of breaking God's law. In that case, according to the law, he could have her killed. There was no way he was doing that. That would be awful.

Joseph stared at the ceiling. He wanted to do the right thing and honour God in all his choices. But which choice was the right one? Maybe he could break off their relationship quietly. Maybe he could just not marry her. Yes. That would probably be his choice. He would just not marry her.

He pulled his blanket tight under his chin. His thoughts continued to spin around in his mind as he sank into an exhausted sleep.

He dreamed.

In his dream, an angel of God stood in front of him, shining with the wonderfulness of God. Gentle and strong, the angel spoke in a voice that was pure truth: 'Joseph, son of David, do not be afraid to get married. The baby inside Mary is from the Holy Spirit. She will give birth to a little boy, and you are to name him Jesus. He will save his people from their sins.'

Joseph opened his eyes. He saw nothing in the blackness of his room, but his chest felt warm, as if God's hand was still on him. He knew that this was more than just a dream. As he lay there, he felt the same lightness and peace that he felt whenever he heard the scriptures read at the synagogue. This dream was real. It was truth from God.

He lay still in bed and thought about everything the angel had said. The baby. Mary's baby. He was a gift from God? Did that mean Mary hadn't broken God's law after all? Did it mean God had *given her* the baby? And the baby would grow up and save people from their sins?

Joseph started to laugh with relief and happiness. Then suddenly a new thought jumped in his mind. He was being asked to be a dad to God's own Son. How would he ever be good enough to do that?

Joseph rolled out of bed and on to his knees. 'Oh, God, I will serve you with my whole heart and life. Thank you for the gift of Jesus. I will become Mary's husband, and I will try to be the best father I can be to the child you are sending to save us all.'

Tears streamed down Joseph's face. What a night it had been!

Joseph smiled and thought back to how worried he had been before he fell asleep. So many choices were swirling around in his mind back then. He had even decided to separate from Mary and not marry her at all.

But now! Now he *would* marry her! He was going to be involved in one of the greatest and most important events in the history of the world—the coming of the Messiah who would save people from their sins. One dream from God can make all the difference in the world.

Extras for parents

Key truth: God speaks truth in the night.

Discussion

If you want to discuss this story with your children, here are some suggestions.

First, help your children recognise the key truth from the story. These questions will help you get started:

- Why was Joseph upset?
- Did Joseph believe what he heard about Mary? Was it true?
- Before he went to sleep, what did he decide to do?
- What truth did God tell Joseph in the dream?
- When he woke up after hearing God's truth, what did he decide to do?

You may want to continue the discussion and broaden your children's understanding of the story's key truth. Choose one or two of these questions to launch a conversation and see where it goes:

- Is it wrong to change your mind about something?
- There was no way Joseph could have been sure of that information about Mary. Only God could have convinced him. Do you think you would have believed God if you were Joseph?
- Sometimes we're not sure what the truth is or what to do, and that makes it hard for us to sleep. What would be helpful to do when we are confused about the truth and are lying in bed at night?

Pray

If you want to pray with your children, here is a prayer that may serve as a starting point.

Father God, thank you that you know all truth and are never confused. Sometimes we don't know what the truth is, God, and that feels frustrating and upsetting. We want to live always with your truth in our lives. As we lie down in our beds with you, God, show us the truth about our worries, so that we can be like Joseph and make decisions based on your truth, not our confusion. Thank you, God.

If you want to help your children connect with God and continue chatting with him on their own, here is a suggestion.

• Invite your children to spend some time alone with God, telling him all about a situation that is frustrating or confusing. Encourage them to be open to hear what God may communicate back.

'Parenting for faith' tool

As our children become more aware of their dreams and the possibility of hearing from God in them, we can become concerned about how to help our children process those dreams. As we know, not all dreams are from God.

Some of your children's dreams will be just normal silly dreams, and you will feel free to talk with your children casually about them and then dismiss them as a part of everyday life.

Some dreams, like Pharaoh's, may feel strange but also important. If your child has a dream like that and has written it down, both of you can chat with God about it and ask him questions about it. The two of you can search in the Bible for anything that looks similar. Most of all, though, don't worry about it. The process of learning God's communication is a lifelong journey, and it is a wonderful experience for a child to learn how to grow in the normal process of life with God. Sometimes, just leaving the dream written down somewhere is good enough, and you can come back to it at a later point.

Some dreams are definitely God-dreams. You will find that if a dream is from God, your child will know it, and it will seem very obvious to you, too. One child I worked with dreamed of God walking in front of her as she went to school. As the other children in her dream threw unkind words at her, the words stuck to God and didn't hurt her at all. When she woke up, she felt safe and happy, knowing that God was with her at school. Her parents were very sure that this was a God-dream.

The important thing to remember is to keep the topic of dreams light. Dreams are only one small aspect of all that God has for us in the night, so we can delight in what God is doing and not become overly focused on any one aspect of dreams. You are the parent, and God will give you discernment. He will work in partnership with you faithfully.

16

A new kind of call

Acts 16

Timothy added a fresh log to the warm fire crackling bright against the moonless night. In the distance was the little seaside town called Troas. 'So what do you think?' asked Timothy. 'Do you think Troas is where we're going to stay for a while?'

Paul and Silas smiled at each other. They had been serving God together for so long and had been through so much together. Timothy was new to their group, still trying to figure out what life on a missionary trip would be like.

Silas turned over the fish cooking on the open fire. 'I truly don't know if Troas is our next spot, Timothy. We will see.'

Paul chuckled. 'After we left Derbe, I was convinced we were going to Asia to tell the people there about Jesus, but, as you know, the Holy Spirit stopped us. So we kept going to Bithynia and I thought *that* was our next place, but... nope. The Spirit wouldn't let us go there either.'

Timothy's forehead crinkled. 'So we're going to Troas because God said "no" to the other places?'

'We're going to Troas because it makes sense,' said Silas. 'It seems the next logical thing to do. Sometimes God guides us by letting us continue on our journey, and then he opens new opportunities for us along the way.'

Paul thumped Timothy's back with a teasing smile. 'That's how we found you! We were asked by the council in Jerusalem to travel around delivering their message, and we followed the open doors and eventually stumbled upon you. God gave us such peace at every step, and we are grateful to have you with us.'

'Thanks. I'm grateful, too,' said Timothy. He stared into the flames and seemed to be thinking. 'So then... why doesn't God just tell us exactly where to go?'

'Sometimes he does,' said Paul. 'Sometimes God makes himself very clear, so clear that you know the name of the person you're supposed to talk to and the street to find them in. I first met Jesus after he'd gone back to heaven. His light and voice were so powerful that they knocked me off my feet. He told me exactly which house to go to and who to ask for. Sometimes he is that specific.'

Silas pulled the sizzling fish off the fire and, after a deep sniff, began to parcel out the food. The three men ate quietly, looking at the sparkling lights of Troas in the distance. The fire continued to snap and pop. Thin curls of smoke twisted up to the night sky.

'God is faithful to guide in many ways,' said Paul, quietly. 'It's just a matter of being ready for it.'

Later that night, Paul closed his eyes and listened to his friends' snores as they lay around the dwindling fire. The smell of the nearby sea drifted in. All of a sudden, a picture of a man appeared in Paul's mind. He had never seen this man before, so he knew it wasn't a memory. The man was wearing white robes, covered by a red coat with beautiful patterns and tassels. He had olive skin and dark hair and was standing tall. The man had his hands in front of him, begging for something.

Paul knew in this moment, in this vision, that God was telling him something. So he kept waiting and watching the picture of the man in his mind. Soon the man spoke. He said, 'Come over to Macedonia and help us. Come over to Macedonia and help us.' Then the picture disappeared.

Paul sat up and smiled at his snoozing friends. He circled around the fire and woke up Silas and Timothy. 'Guys, I've had a vision from God. Tell me what you think!' Paul stirred the fire until it was crackling again. In its warm glow, Paul told Timothy and Silas about his vision.

'It feels right,' said Silas. 'The people in Macedonia need to hear the good news of Jesus as much as anyone. If God is saying go there, then we'll go!'

'How do we get there?' asked Timothy.

Paul grinned, then winked at Timothy. 'Well, you will never guess. You see that town Troas right there? It's a place where we can get a boat straight to Macedonia.' Paul leapt up and began to gather his bedding.

'So are you saying that, without us knowing it, God actually led us here? So we can get to the *next* place he's sending us?' Timothy looked in wonder at the sleepy town in front of them.

The three men laughed and laughed as they packed their stuff together. As the sun rose, they walked into Troas, confident in God's guidance and plan. God's vision in the night was all they needed to step into the next exciting adventure with him.

Extras for parents

Key truth: God guides us in the night.

Discussion

If you want to discuss this story with your children, here are some suggestions.

First, help your children recognise the key truth from the story. These questions will help you get started:

- Why were Paul and his friends travelling from town to town?
- Why had they not found a new town to stay in yet?
- How did God guide Paul and his friends at night?

You may want to continue the discussion and broaden your children's understanding of the story's key truth. Choose one or two of these questions to launch a conversation and see where it goes:

- Sometimes, when we don't know what to do, we just stop. Why did Paul and his friends keep going? Did Paul expect to hear from God that night?
- God guided Paul and his friends in a different way from the one they expected. How do you think they felt about that?
- Paul was just resting when God gave him the picture of the man from Macedonia. What do you think Paul did at bedtime, to be ready for God to do that?

Pray

If you want to pray with your children, here is a prayer that may serve as a starting point.

Father God, thank you that you guide us in our lives. We want to have great adventures with you, and we want to be a small part of your wonderful plans here on earth. Please make our night-times full of your love and guidance, so that we will always be close to you. Thank you, God.

If you want to help your children connect with God and continue chatting with him on their own, here are a few suggestions to help them sum up this experience of focusing on the night-time:

- Tell your children a story of when God guided you, and ask if they have a situation in their life where they need God's help to know what to do next. Ask them to chat to God about it, and provide some space for them to receive God's communication. Encourage your children that God's guidance comes in many ways, just as it did for Paul and his friends. Assure them that you can all keep talking about how God is guiding them over the next days and weeks.
- Flick through this book with your children and let them point out their favourite story from the whole book. Encourage them to take a moment to connect with God right now and chat with him about why that was their favourite story of the night-time.
- Chat with your children about the next steps in their night-time journey with God. Suggest that they each make a plan with God about how they want to do night-times in the future. The following evening, chat about what they and God have decided.

'Parenting for faith' tool

Night-time with God is a wonderful gift that you can give your children. As you have been reading this book to them, you have been giving them tools for thinking about God and connecting with him in the night. These truths will last a long time.

The best 'parenting for faith' tool you have is your own partnership between you and God. As you continue on your journey of parenting children to know and love him, be encouraged to know that the God who created the night and meets with you in it will be covering you and connecting with you in your nights as well.

Frequently Asked Questions

THERE WERE A LOT OF KEY TRUTHS IN THE BOOK. HOW DO I HELP MY CHILD REMEMBER THEM ALL?

This book covers 16 key truths about God in the night, but you and your family will discover many more on your own. Many families have found it useful to create a visual reminder of these key truths, something that parents and children can all use as they get ready for bed. I know a lot of parents who are great at crafts. Here are a few of their inspiring projects.

- Make pillowcase reminders. Every night, after you have read a story, let each child write the new key truth on to a pillowcase using fabric pens. By the end of the book, each child will have a pillowcase covered with key truths about who God is and what he does in the night.
- Make a duvet cover reminder. Your child can draw pictures on a duvet cover of her favourite parts of the stories, to help her remember what God can do in the night-time.
- Make a notebook reminder. Your child can decorate the cover of a blank notebook, filling it with reminders of the key truths. The notebook can then become your child's bedtime book, and in it he can write his thoughts, prayers and worries to God. It will be his special notebook for communication between him and God.
- Make a notecard reminder. At a family night, let each person decorate a small card and write the list of key truths on it, starting with 'Tonight, God…' Each person can place their card next to their bed or on their dressing-table and use it as a reminder.

It is most important to keep these reminders as a part of your night-time conversations and refer to them often. These truths about God's character and actions are always relevant. As life continues moving forward and new night-time situations emerge, these reminders will help your children remember the truth of who God is in the night.

THERE ARE SO MANY THINGS IN THE WORLD THAT MAKE MY CHILD AFRAID AT NIGHT AND GIVE HIM FEARS AND NIGHTMARES—TELEVISION SHOWS, HORROR FILM POSTERS, AND EVEN HALLOWEEN DISCUSSIONS AT SCHOOL. IS ALL OF THAT INEVITABLE? OR SHOULD I BE STOPPING MY CHILD FROM SEEING THINGS THAT MAY POP UP LATER AND SCARE HIM AT NIGHT-TIME?

The answer is 'yes' to both questions. Yes, it is our responsibility to guard our children's minds and hearts. But yes, we will never be able to fully control the world around our children.

Our job is to protect our children and train them in how to make wise decisions about living in the world. So when it comes to things we can control, like television and films, games and media, it is our job to set the boundaries. Simply saying, 'I don't want those scary pictures in your brain. I only want things that make you feel strong and good in your brain' can frame for your children the choices you are making. Or you can say, 'Scary stories make you forget about the truth of how powerful God is and where he is in the night-time. I don't like things that make you forget about the truth.'

You can also chat about how God designed us for peace; he didn't design us for fear. So when television programmes or films begin to make us feel afraid or anxious, it's like poison to our hearts and we need to stop feeding it in.

Our goal is to raise children to have soft hearts towards God and the ability to monitor themselves. We need to equip them to make decisions for themselves and to know how to deal with the scary things that pop up in their minds. Share stories of times when you accidentally let some bad pictures or stories into your brain, and how they affected you. Talk about how you dealt with them with God, and what you learned about how to deal with those images when they popped up.

MY CHILD IS AFRAID OF THE DARK, AND HE INSISTS THERE ARE MONSTERS IN HIS ROOM OR GHOSTS IN THE HALLWAY. SETTLING HIM TAKES AGES. HE CALLS FOR ME OFTEN, AND HE WANTS ME TO LEAVE A LOT OF LIGHTS ON. HOW DO I HELP HIM STOP BEING AFRAID?

In this scenario we often try to use logic with our children or attempt to prove that their fear is unfounded. We turn on lights, explain what the scary shadow is, and try to reason with their fear. While that may be helpful in the moment, it doesn't address the underlying issue that our child is feeling vulnerable and unsafe.

We have to remember that being afraid in the dark is logical. We cannot see around us, so we cannot feel totally sure that we are safe from harm. Naturally, we become more alert to sounds and to shadows as our brains search for anything dangerous. When children combine this natural fear with their natural imaginations, they may experience anything from slight unease to paralysing fear.

Our children's solution in this situation is to call for us. When we enter the room, they know that we are stronger and more powerful than whatever they are afraid of. They feel safe with us, so the fear goes away. Their fear goes away because they are changing their focus from the thing that is making them afraid to the one who makes them feel safe. We need to give our children the ability to change their focus to God, the one who is more powerful than anyone or anything; the one who will never leave them.

You have already laid a foundation for that ability by reading through this book with your children. Now it is a matter of empowering them to learn how to refocus themselves on God instead of on their fear.

First, I suggest that you and your child make a toolbox of items or activities that work particularly well in connecting her to God or reminding her of the key truths. They might be a journal, a worship CD, a pad of paper to draw on, a Bible to read, a copy of the list of key truths, and a small torch.

Then, I suggest that you try a several-step process that will fit your family. It might look like this.

- The first time she calls and is afraid, you go in and pray with her.
- The second time she calls, you do not go in, but you encourage her to chat with God about her fear and catch what he has to say about it. Tell your child that you know she and God will figure it out.
- The third time she calls, you do not go in, but you encourage her to try one of the activities from her toolbox.
- After ten minutes of silence, pop your head in to check on the progress.

The goal is for your child to grow in confidence that, on her own, she can connect with God, trust in him and find peace with him. It may take a while for your child to get there, and your steps may be different from those listed above. Remember, your plan is to ease your child into focusing on God, and not on the fear.

MY FOUR-YEAR-OLD OFTEN TELLS ME THAT GOD HAS TOLD HIM THINGS OR DONE THINGS TOGETHER WITH HIM IN HIS DREAMS. WHAT SHOULD I DO?

It is wonderful when our children feel that God is connecting with them in their sleep. As parents, though, we want to help our children learn to tell the difference between what is of God and what isn't.

I suggest that we help children to ask three questions to see if their dream is specifically God-given.

- Does it sound like God? Does it line up with what we know about God from the Bible?
- How does it make us feel? Or what is the 'fruit'? If it makes us feel condemned or afraid, or if it makes us want to run away or hide from God, it isn't from him. We know that God always wants us to come towards him and feel loved. If it pushes us away from God, then it isn't from him.
- What do wise people think about it? God put us in community to help each other. If we are not sure, we can chat with other people who can help us.

Once there was a five-year-old boy who had a dream that he and God were playing together, and then lots of 'baddie ninjas' came and tried to attack him. God stepped in front of the boy, and then, all of a sudden, God shone so brightly that the baddie ninjas fell down in front of him, saying, 'Holy, holy, holy.' The boy woke up feeling really excited.

His mum helped him to process the dream by saying, 'Wow! How do you feel?' The boy confidently replied, 'I know that if anything tries to hurt me, I should just stand behind God, and he will shine and defeat all the baddies.' The mum nodded and said, 'In the Bible, someone else saw God and described him as being as bright as the sun, just like you did. That person also said that one day everyone will worship God, just the way you told me. Thanks for telling me about your dream. I love hearing what you and God do together at night.'

If the dream doesn't line up with the three questions above, you have a great opportunity to help your children learn what to do with it. With older children, you can coach them through the questions and assess the dream together. With younger ones, feel free to make the assessment as a parent and say, 'That sounds like a very vivid dream, but I wouldn't worry about it. I don't think it was a God-dream, because look how scared you are. God would never send you a dream just to scare you. Let's just put that dream in a box and kick it out of our head, because nothing gets to stay in your head that isn't right with God.'

MY CHILD HAS BAD DREAMS AND KEEPS ASKING ME WHY GOD DOESN'T TAKE THE BAD DREAMS AWAY. WHAT DO I TELL HER?

Bad dreams happen to all of us. They can be absolutely awful for children, and for us, as parents, to hear about. Our children can feel powerless to stop them, and that leads to frustration and fear.

I find it helpful to explain to children that, while we sleep, our brains are doing amazing things. Our brains are storing our memories and processing everything we have learned. They are resetting our bodies for the next day and making sense of all we experienced the day before. Sometimes, when we have bad dreams, it's just our brains telling us that something scared us, or something made us stressed or anxious about tomorrow.

That doesn't mean the dreams aren't frightening. Of course they are. But we can chat with God about our bad dreams, and he can do lots of things in the night that will help. We can look together at key truths of what God does in the night, and we can use the tools we've learned about connecting with God, to chat with him about what we are feeling and what we need.

We can also use our tools to help us become more peaceful by turning our thoughts away from our fear and towards the wonderful things of life and God, so that we can get back to sleep. When we are worshipping God, praying, chatting with him, or using whatever is in our toolbox, we are continually strengthening our connection with God in the night.

As parents, it is always helpful to be connecting with God on our own as we guide our children through this experience. The Bible says that if we lack wisdom, we only need to ask for it. When it comes to our children's fears, God will guide us with his wisdom, so that we can perceive what is behind our children's thoughts and fears, and support them well.

Parenting for Faith

Did you find *Comfort in the Darkness* helpful in encouraging your children to draw close to God and find comfort at night? We want to continue supporting you on your journey of Parenting for Faith!

Parenting for Faith is part of The Bible Reading Fellowship (BRF). BRF is passionate about making a difference through the Christian faith, and we are seeing lives and communities transformed through the Parenting for Faith approach that Rachel Turner has developed. We are seeking to inspire and support you as you spiritually parent your children, connecting you with the Parenting for Faith community and a variety of resources. We want to encourage you and cheer you on the great adventure of parenting your children and teens for faith.

Find out more and join the conversation at
www.parentingforfaith.org.

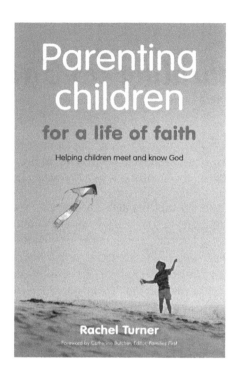

Parenting Children for a Life of Faith explores how the home can become the primary place in which children are nurtured into the reality of God's presence and love, equipped to access him themselves and encouraged to grow in a two-way relationship with him that will last a lifetime. We need to model for our children what it means to be in a relationship with God rather than just equipping them to know about him—helping our children to be God-connected rather than just God-smart.

Parenting Children for a Life of Faith
Helping children meet and know God
Rachel Turner
978 1 84101 607 8 £7.99

brfonline.org.uk

Parenting Children for a Life of Purpose is a practical and tested handbook exploring the possibilities for helping children to discover the specific gifts for whatever God is calling them to be. It shows how parents might work in partnership with churches to enable children to find their true identity and purpose in life.

Parenting Children for a Life of Purpose
Empowering children to become who they are called to be
Rachel Turner
978 0 85746 163 6 £7.99

brfonline.org.uk

The world has a formula for confidence: 'You are amazing and perfect, just the way you are. People should love and accept you, and, if they don't, well, that's their problem.' We may think that if our children could just believe those statements deep in their hearts, then they would be confident and joyful. The problem is that the formula doesn't work. In this thought-provoking and engaging book Rachel Turner explores how we can help our children to discover a healthy core of confidence, offering practical wisdom and suggestions for nurturing it in daily life.

Parenting Children for a Life of Confidence
Releasing children to live in God's strength
Rachel Turner
978 0 85746 167 4 £8.99

brfonline.org.uk

BRF

Transforming
lives and communities

Christian growth and understanding of the Bible

Resourcing individuals, groups and leaders in churches for their own spiritual journey and for their ministry

Church outreach in the local community

Offering three programmes that churches are embracing
to great effect as they seek to engage
with their local communities
and transform lives

Teaching Christianity in primary schools

Working with children and teachers to explore Christianity creatively and confidently

Children's and family ministry

Working with churches and families to explore Christianity creatively and bring the Bible alive

The Bible Reading Fellowship (BRF) is a Registered Charity (No. 233280)